AF211145

**First edition**
**Copyright © 2015 Saiwan Kamber**
**Published & Printed by: BoD**
**ISBN: 9789174638387**
**www.feyli.se**
**Info@feyli.se**

To my dear parents
Jasim and Lamieh, my heroes.
And to my beloved daughter Madjan.

**Acknowledgments**
**I would like to thank the following people for their help**
**with shaping this book**

**Jasim Kamber**
**Lamieh Say**
**Ebrahim Jahanbakhsh**

# Foreword

The purpose of this book is to give the reader an insight into the proverbs used within the Feyli dialect of Kurdish. Furthermore, it is a way to preserve and propagate the Feyli dialect.

The book begins with an explanation of how the Latin letters are used. In order to preserve the correct pronunciation and prevent misunderstandings, each word is written exactly as they sound. I believe it to be of outmost importance since there are words that sound very similar to each other but have different meanings.

To ensure that the proverbs spirit is not lost, I haven't always translated them word for word.
Where necessary, I have added additional comments for the proverbs to be understood correctly. The comments can be found below the English translation in [].
The book ends with a glossary consisting of "difficult" words.

Happy reading.

# Feylî alphabet

| Letter | Example | Pronunciation |
|--------|---------|---------------|
| **A, a** | **A**gir (Fire), **A**yim (Human) | T(**a**)ll |
| **B, b** | **B**ar (Burden), **B**aL (Wing, Arm) | (**B**)ig |
| **C, c** | **C**ûwan (Young), **C**î (Place) | (**J**)ohn |
| **Ç ç** | **Ç**eft (Askew), **Ç**ew (Eye) | (**Ch**)apter |
| **D, d** | **D**ar (Tree), **D**aLig (Mother) | (**D**)ay |
| **E, e** | **E**ncîr (Fig), **E**ger (If) | B(**a**)d, Swedish Ä |
| **Ê, ê** | **Ê**ware (Dusk), R**ê** (Road) | Th(**e**)re |
| **F, f** | **F**irye (Much/Very), **F**îl (Elephant) | (**F**)ree |
| **G, g** | **G**iran (Expensive), **G**ep (Big) | (**G**)reat |
| **H, h** | **H**eşt (Eight), **H**awsa (Neighbour) | (**H**)appy |
| **I, i** | **I**ncig (Clothes), **I**msaL (This year) | B(**i**)t |
| **Î, î** | **Î**la (This side), S**î**r (Garlic) | Fr(**ee**) |
| **J, j** | **J**an (Pain), **J**in (Woman) | French **J** |
| **K, k** | **K**ew (Blue), **K**awirr (Sheep) | (**K**)ey |
| **L, l** | **L**iç (Lip), **L**ifane (Twin/Pair) | (**L**)ife |
| **M, m** | **M**ar (Snake), **M**aL (House) | (**M**)ercy |

| | | |
|---|---|---|
| **N, n** | **N**an (Bread), **N**ixan (Nail) | (N)ew |
| **O, o** | K**o**me (Many), M**o**re (Nut) | English **O** |
| **P, p** | **P**a (Leg), **P**ül (Money) | (P)luralistic |
| **Q, q** | **Q**ert (Loan), **Q**eün (Fat) | Arabic **Q** in Ira(**q**) |
| **R, r** | **R**ê (Road), **R**as (Truth/Right) | (R)ose |
| **S, s** | **S**a (Shadow), **S**aL (Year) | (S)trength |
| **Ş, ş** | **Ş**an (Shoulder), **Ş**ar (City) | (Sh)ape |
| **T, t** | **T**aze (New/Fresch), **T**ûp (Ball) | (T)ruth |
| **U, u** | K**u**rr (Boy), K**u**L (Short) | Sh(o)rt |
| **Û, û** | K**û**r (Blind), K**û**L (Shoulder) | B(oo)th |
| **V, v** | Gî**v** (Diameter), Mid**v**er (Roe deer) | (V)ery |
| **W, w** | **W**aran (Rain), **W**ehar (Spring) | (W)ill |
| **X, x** | **X**aLû (Uncle), **X**aw (Sleep/Dream) | (Kh)an |
| **Y, y** | **Y**ek (One), **Y**e (This) | (Y)ellow |
| **Z, z** | **Z**êw (Ground/Earth), **Z**ûr (Strength) | (Z)ebra |

The author assumes the Kurmancî alphabet (ü is an exception).

The reader will also find capital letter L in some of the words. These L's correspond to the American L in App(L)e and (L)eg. It is pronounced normally when in the beginning of a word.

There are two other ways to write L => ll and ł. As there are no standard to follow, the author has chosen L.
Letters that are repeated stresses the letter. For example **Kirr, Wirr, Xirr**.

# A

**Adetê daştî le şîrî – Terkê nîyekey le pîrî**
ئادەتێ داشتی لە شیری – تەرکێ نییەکەی لە پیری
A habit learned as a child – Can't be getting rid of when old

**Agir bê dükeL nîyew**
ئاگر بێ دۆکەڵ نییەو
No fire without smoke

**Agir ki keftew, terr u hişk neyrê**
ئاگر ک کەفتەو، تەڕ و هشک نەیرێ
The burning fire distinguishes not between wet and dry

**Agir we agir nîyekujyêdew**
ئاگر وە ئاگر نییەکوژیێدەو
One can not extinguish fire with fire

**Agir xase dem u dü, bira xase ne çü şü**
ئاگر خاسە دەم و دۆ، برا خاسە نە چۆ شۆ
Fire is well, lit or smoky, brother is good but not as the husband

**AqiL we işare, nezan we kutek**
ئاقڵ وە ئشارە، نەزان وە کوتەک
The wise with a nod, the stupid with a cudgel

**Aqiweti ziLm kirdin, cewr kîşane**
ئاقوەت زڵم کردن، جەور کیشانە
Misery is the evildoer's salary

**Ard de teyre qert key?**

ئارد ده تهیره قهرت کهی؟

Do you borrow flour from a thief?

**Ardi berü le tîwiLê nîyewisê**

ئارد بهرۆ له تیولێ نییهوسێ

Chestnut flour does not stick to his forehead

**Ardi naw dirrig (Dirrigi naw ard)**

ئارد ناو درگ

Flour among thorns

[Confused]

**Aşi çill kêwanû**

ئاش چل کێوانوو

Forty (old) women's soup

[Too many cooks spoil the broth]

**Asin we jengi xwey darizyêd**

ئاسن وه ژهنگ خوهی دارزیێد

Iron rots of its own rust

[One who creates his own problems]

**Asîyaw girrmey tîyey u ardê dîyar nîye**

ئاسییاو گرمهی تییهی و ئاردێ دییار نییه

There are a lot of noises from the mill, but no flour is showing

[Much ado about nothing]

**Aw le asîyaweyl keft u deng u bas temam bü (Aw le asîyaw bikefê)**

ئاو له ئاسییاوهیل کهفت و دهنگ و باس تهمام بۆ

When the water flows in the water mill all discussions stops

**Aw le desi narijyê**

ئاو له دهسێ نارژیێ

Water doesn't drip through his fingers

[Stingy]


**Aw le yê cî bimêni genyê**

ئاو له یێ جی بمێنێ گەنیێ

Stagnant water stinks


**Aw u agir mawiL neyrin**

ئاو و ئاگر ماوڵ نەیرن

Water and fire gives you no respite


**Aw we peLe we qert nîyeyd**

ئاو وه پەڵه وه قەرت نییەید

He does not borrow water to the monsoon (autumn rain)


**Aw wisya tu newis**

ئاو وسیا تو نەوس

If the water stops, don't you!


**Awi jîrê key**

ئاو ژیرێ کەی

The water under hay

[Hidden intent]


**Awê ki rişya cemew nîyewd (Awig rişya girdew nîyew)**

ئاوێ ک رشیا جەمەو نییەود

One can not collect spilled water


7

**Awi zûrdar werew biLênî çû**

ئاو زووردار وەرەو بڵێنی چوو

Strong waterflow, flows upward

**Awman we yê cû nîyeçû**

ئاومان وە یێ جوو نییەچوو

Our water does not run into the same river

[Does not get along]

**Awi zel deyd?**

ئاو زەل دەید؟

Do you water the reed?

[Meaningless work]

**Axiri yarî cenge, axiri dûsî dujmenî**

ئاخر یاری جەنگە، ئاخر دووسی دوژمەنی

Helpfulness ends with brawl, friendship ends with enmity

**Ayimi qeün; Mirdin u le qewr nanê (naninê) gene**

ئایمێ قەۆن؛ مردن و لە قەور نانێ (ناننێ) گەنه

A fat man´s death and his burial is painful

**Ayim firexwer du car mirê**

ئایم فرەخوەر دو جار مرێ

The gluttonous dies twice

**Ayim ta le esp nekefê espsiwarî yad nîyegrê (Sûwar ta nerrimê, sûwarî yay nîyegrê)**

ئایم تا لە ئەسپ نەکەفێ ئەسپسواری یاد نییەگرێ

As long as you have not fallen off the horse, you will not learn how to ride

8

**Ayim xweş-hisaw, şerîk maL merdime**

ئايم خوەش ھساو، شەریک مأڵ مەردمه

The generous one has part in peoples homes

# B

**Bari çeft ta maL narisi (Bari çeft we menziL nîyeçû)**

بار چەفت تا مأڵ نارسێ

A crooked load do not arrive at destination

**Biçme cayg kesmeşnasê, ewqerge dirû bidem pirr kirwasi (Biçim we şarê kesim nenasê – Wesfi xwem bikem pirr kirwasê)**

بچمه جایگ کەسمەشناسێ، ئەوقەرگه دروو بدەم پڕ کرواسێ

If I visit a new place, I'll lie a dress full

**Bira mar bê, he hizar bê! (Bira eger mar bû, hizar bû)**

برا مار بێ، هه هزار بێ!

If one's brother is a snake, may he be in the thousands!

**Bar era pîya, tewn era jin**

بار ئەرا پییا، تەون ئەرا ژن

Burden for man, weaving for woman

**Bani çewê birüye neyrê**

بان چەوێ برۆیه نەیرێ

There are no eyebrows over her eyes

**Bawgi bîbira u amûzay fire**

باوگ بی برا و ئامووزای فره

Brotherless father and many cousins (Father's brother's children!)

[No help when you needed it, now when no help is needed, there are plenty of helping hands]


**Barîkew bû, beLam nawiryê (nîyewiryey)**

باریکهو بوو، وهڵام ناورێی

It becomes thin but does not snap

[Patience]


**Bawg kur xwey nasêd**

باوگ کور خوهی ناسێد

A father knows his son


**Bawg beLa, daLig qeza – Jin nêmet xuda**

باوگ بهڵا،دالگ قهزا – ژن نێمهت خودا

Lousy mother and father – Wife, godsend


**Bawgi pîye xwer, kuri kewaw xwer**

باوگ پییهخوهر، کور کهواو خوهر

Fat eating father, meat eating son

[As below]


**Bawgi gûşt mexwer kuri qesaw xeydew**

باوگ گووشت مهخوهر کور قهساو خهيدهو

A vegetarian father, raises the butcher's son


**Bawgim xas bû, daLigim düyeti merdime**

باوگم خاس بوو، دالگم دۆیهت مهردمه

As long as my father is a good father, my mother is someone's daughter


10

**Bawg mirdê xefê, le wirsî mirdê nîyexefê**

باوگ مردێ خەفێ، لە ورسی مردێ نیيەخەفێ

The one whose father has died sleeps, the dead can not sleep because of hunger

[The concern for daily bread never disappear]


**Bawejin bawgi bimrê, birajin biray bimrê**

باوەژن باوگێ بمرێ، براژن بر ای بمرێ

May stepmother's father die, may sister in law's brother die

[To ask God for something illogical]


**Bira erê rûji teng, tifeng erê rûji ceng**

برا ئەرێ رووژ تەنگ، تفەنگ ئەرێ رووژ جەنگ

Friend for difficult days, rifle for days of war


**Bira biray mine, tu tarîfi keyd?**

بر ا بر ای منه، تو تاریفێ کەید؟

It's MY brother, why are YOU talking about him in good terms?


**Birat, herçê dirat**

بر ات، هەرچێ در ات

Your brother, whatever it became


**Birayman birayî, kîseman cîyay (Birame bira, kîseman cîya)**

بر ایمان بر ایی، کیسەمان جییای

Friendship is one thing, my money another


**Birinc we demi nîyefîsê**

برنج وه دەمێ نیيەفيسێ

Rice doesn't soak in his mouth

**Bizan u meke**

بزان و مەکە

Know and don't

**Bawanî düyeti necar tûkiLaşe**

باوانی دۆیەت نەجار تووکلاشه

Carpenter's daughters' dowry is wood chip

**Bizin erê şewig, cî xwey xweş keyd**

بزن ئەرئ شەوگ، جی خوەی خوەش کەید

The goat arranges his abode even for a night

**Büçigî bike, ta gewrayg bayde şanid**

بۆچگی بکە، تا گەورایگ بایده شاند

Be humble, so the esteemed one make you company

**Bûd ew la xirsege bûm?**

بوود ئەو لا خرسەگه بووم؟

Does it make sense to help the bear?
[Helping his enemy]

**Berd eray merde (Pîyag)**

بەرد ئەرای مەرده

Stone is for men

**Beşker beşê kird, xwey we wirsî men**

بەشکەر بەشئ کرد، خوەی وه ورسی مەن

The distributor distributed, he himself ended up with nothing

**Be le gerdene we insaf**

به له گەردەنه وه ئنساف

Punish fairly

**Bê xûwî erê ayim lîwe bike**

بێ خووی ئەرێ ئايم لیوه بکه

To perform a good deed for a crazy person!

**Bîkarî kargay şeytane**

بیکاری کارگای شەیتانه

Idleness is the devil's workshop

**Bîgar büd, bîkar newd/neüd**

بیگار بۆد، بیکار نەود

Be idle but not unemployed

**Bîla barim xalî bikem, ewsa büş encîre ya enare**

بیلا بارم خالی بکەم، ئەوسا بۆش ئەنجیره یا ئەناره

Allow me to empty my load, then ask if it's fig or pomegranate

**Bîhûde xerid we çen?**

بیهووده خەرد وه چەن؟

How much do you pay for useless things?

**Bê le wey, ta çinar bilerzê**

بێ له وەی، تا چنار بلەرزێ

Hit the ash so the maple tremble

**Bira, biramid - Jin xwastid hewsamid**

برا، برامد ـ ژن خواستد هەوسامد

In friendship, you are my friend - when you get married, you are my neighbour

# C

**Cûri nijî wer u pişt neyrê (Çü qeme weri pişt neyrê)**

جوور نژی وەر و پشت نەیری

Like a lentil he has neither a back nor front side

**Cengi pîya u jin bawer pê meke**

جەنگ پییا و ژن باوەر پی مەکه

Do not believe in a brawl between married couples

**Ceng rewyadew, çiLmin we şûni çû gerdê**

جەنگ رەوییادەو، چلمن وه شوون چوو گەردی

The battle has ended, the fool is looking for weapons

**Ceng kirdin xastir le betaLa büne**

جەنگ کردن خاستر له بەتالا بۆنه

Waging war is better than being unemployed

**Ceng le cîye cengan xweşe**

جەنگ له جییه جەنگان خوەشه

War is fun, in the battlefield

**Cehenem we derê biresew, we binê meçû**

جەهەنەم وه دەری برەسەو، وه بنی مەچوو

Arrive to the edge of hell, but do not enter

**Cûwanî pirri guLe, eger bizanî - pîrî bari xeme, eger bitwanî**

جووانی پری گوله، ئەگەر بزانی - پیری باری خەمه، ئەگەر بتوانی

Youth is full of pleasure, if you only knew - Old age is a burden of sorrow, if you are able

**CahiL kûre, xeyr u şerr xwey le yekew nîyekey**

جاهڵ کووره، خەیر و شەڕ خوەی لە یەکەو نییەکەی

Youth is blind; It can not distinguish between good and evil

# Ç

**Çill kes le naw işkeftün, gurg xwardeyan**

چل کەس لە ناو ئشکەفتۆن، گورگ خواردەیان

Forty people were in a cave, a wolf ate them all
[Fear, Cowardice]

**Çiraxig we maL rewas, we mescid herame!**

چراخگ وەتمالّ ڕەهواس، وەتمەسجد هەرامە!

A lamp that is OK for the home, is not allowed in the mosque

**Çi rûjê wefir bû, ew rûje zimsane**

چ ڕووژیٚ وەفر بوو، ئەو ڕووژە زمسانه

The day it snows, that day is winter

**Çiştê ki le maL mîr fires, nan u pîyaze**

چشتیٚ ک لە ماڵ میر فرەس، نان و پییازه

What's plentiful in prince's house is onion and bread

**Çime bawan tekew derim - Xemi dinya kefte serim**

چمه باوان تەکەو دەرم ـ خەم دنیا کەفتە سەرم

I went to my family home to get some rest - I got the world's grief

15

**Çû eLgir, sey diz dîyare**

چوو ئەلّگر ، سەی دز دییاره

Arm yourself, the thief's dog is showing

**Çûwar çişt pîya şiknê: Qerti fire, MinaL fire, Dijmini fire, Jini bîxisLet**

چووار چشت پییا شکنێ: قەرت فره ، منالّ فره ، دژمن فره ، ژن بیخسلّەت

Four things breaks the man: A lot of loans, a lot of children, a lot of enemies, a bad wife

**Çû xuda dengê nîye - Her ke bixwey deway nîye**

چوو خودا دەنگێ نییه هەر که بخوەی دەوای نییه

God's punishment "does not sound" - Those who are afflicted have no cure

**Çü keLeşêr, namewq qülinê**

چۆ کەلّەشێر ، نامەوق قۆلنێ

Just like the rooster, he crows untimely

**Çû le barîkî şikêt, merd le qayimî**

چوو له باریکی شکێت، مەرد له قایمی

A branch breaks of its thinness, a man of his hardness

**Çuner wet serim sûktir, ezawim kemtir**

چونەر وەت سەرم سووکتر ، ئەزاوم کەمتر

The beetroot said: Lighter head, lesser pain

**ÇepLe we yê des nîyekutyê**

چەپلّه وه یێ دەس نییەکوتێ

One can not clap with one hand

**ÇukuLşikin xwey şiknê**

چوکولّشکن خوەی شکنێ

A hypocrite destroys himself

16

**Çeqû miştey xwey nîyewirê**

چەقوو مشتەی خوەی نییەورێ

The knife does not cut its own shank

**Çemya gûçan, neçemya saçû (Er çemya, gûçan. Er neçemya, saçû.)**

چەمیا گووچان، نەچەمیا ساچوو

If it bends (bended handle) stick, if it does not bend (straight) stick

**Çarey xew, xeftine - Çarey rê reftene**

چارەی خەو، خەفتنە چارەی رێ رەفتەنە

Insomnias cure is to sleep, a journeys cure is to walk it

**Çiray feqîr mange şewe**

چرای فەقیر مانگەشەوه

The moon is the poor mans night light

**Çenê lareme, qersequLê barime**

چەنێ لارەمه، قەرسەقوڵێ بارمه

Unhappy me, droppings (donkey's stools) is my load

**Çew bidray, negi naw bidray**

چەو بدرای، نەگ ناو بدرای

May I loose my eye but not my honour

**Çewi diz le çew sawmaL tîjtire**

چەو دز له چەو ساومڵ تیژترە

The thief's eyes are sharper than the owner's

**Çewim dî, diLim ney (nedî)**

چەوم دی، دڵم نەی

He saw my eyes but not my heart

**Çîde xwazmenî, şewekyan biçû**

چیدە خوازمەنی، شەوەکیان بچوو

Are you going to propose, do it in the morning!

**Çîde xwazmenî kesig, Eger dadey pêd xwed we şaqizî mezan! Eger nêyadey pêd xwed we güxwer mezan!**

چیدە خوازمەنی کەسگ، ئەگەر دادەی پێد خوەد وە شاقزی مەزان! ئەگەر نییادەی پێد خوەد وە گۆخوەر مەزان!

When you propose, if you get yes for an answer don't be proud, if you get no for an answer don't feel a fool

# D

**Dar ki berr egri, ser eçemni [Dar berr girê, ser çemnê]**

دار ک بەر ئەگری، سەر ئەچەمنی

When the tree bears fruit, it bends

**Der maLid bûwes, hewsa neke diz**

دەر ماڵد بووەس، هەوسا نەکە دز

Close your door, don't make your neighbour a thief

**Der merdim nekut, derid kutin**

دەر مەردم نەکوت، دەرد کوتن

Do not knock on peoples door, they will knock on yours

**Des şikyay, zewaLi gerdene**

دەس شکیای، زەواڵ گەردەنە

A broken arm is the burden of the neck

**Du bira cen kirdin - Lîwe le û düre bawir kird**

دو برا جەن کردن ـ لیوه لەو دۆره باور کرد

Two brothers fought each other – The fool thought it being for real

**DaLig her meşkeyg bijenê, düyetîş jenêd**

دالْگ هەر مەشکەیگ بژەنێ، دۆیەتیش ژەنێد

The daughter does what her mother does

**Dür le şitir bixef, xaw heLpeLe neywn (Le şitir dür bixef – Xaw heLpeLe neün)**

دۆر لە شتر بخەف، خاو هەڵپەڵە نەیون

Sleep far from the camel, dream no nightmares

[Keep away from dishonest people and avoid problems]

**Dêanê ki êyşa, kîşya**

دێنانێ ک نێشا، کیشیا

The tooth that ached, was pulled out

**Dêan saz kesige we dêan merdim nan xwey**

دێیان ساز کەسگه وه دێیان مەردم نان خوەی

A dentist is one who eats with people's teeth

**Desi tema dirîje**

دەس تەما دریژه

Greed's hand is long

**Desi xwed eray xwed**

دەس خوەد ئەرای خوەد

Your hand for yourself

**Desi petî tûz le lê heLsê?**

دەس پەتی تووز له لێ هەڵسێ؟

Does it dust from an empty hand?

**Desi bêgane tam dîrê**

دەس بێگانه تام دیرێ

The stranger's hand is tasty

[The grass is always greener on the other side]

**Derekî hat binekî der kird**

دەرەکی هات بنەکی دەر کرد

The stranger came and threw out the native

**Der le bani paşne çerxê**

دەر له بان پاشنه چەرخێ

The door turns on its hinges

**Düyetid bê(d)e jin mirdê - Manga bê(d)e ga birdê**

دۆیەتد بێیه ژن مردێ ـ مانگا بێیه گا بردێ

Let your daughter marry a widower – Give your cow to one whose cow has died

**Dûs le bana(w) nûrrê, dişmen le jêra(w)**

دووس له بانا نوورێ، دشمەن له ژێرا

A friend sees you from above, an enemy from below

**Dûsî bîcehet bû, dişmenî bîcehet nîyew**

دووسی بیجەهەت بوو، دشمەنی بیجەهەت نییەو

Friendship without cause is possible, enmity without cause is impossible

**Dür bû, dûs bû**

دۆر بوو، دووس بوو

Be distant, be appreciated

20

**Dikandar heLeLe key, herçê le dikanê bû**

دکاندار هەڵەڵە کەی، هەرچیٰ لە دکانیٰ بوو

A shopkeeper advertises no matter what he has in his store


**Dijmin mirê, rîşey nîyemirê**

دژمن مریٰ، ریشەی نییەمریٰ

The enemy dies, its root consists


**Dizê ki le diz bidizê, şa-dize**

دزیٰ ک لە دز بدزیٰ، شا دزه

A thief who steals from other thieves is the king of thieves


**Diz xweşye, bazar şêwyay**

دز خوەشیه، بازار شیٰویای

The thief rejoices when there is turmoil in the Bazaar


**Dan le deri qingi, wet: Ay diganim**

دان لە دەر قنگیٰ، وەت: ئای دگانم

They spanked him in the butt, he cried: My tooth!


**DaLig wet: Mi mirim - Düyet wet: Mi şü kem**

دالٝگ وەت: م مرم - دۆیەت وەت: م شۆ کەم

The mother said: I am dying - The daughter said: I am getting married


**DaLigid bimrê, ard u aw**

دالٝگد بمریٰ، ئارد و ئاو

When your mother dies, flour and water

**DaLigi diz ya sîne xwey(exwad) ya sîne kutê**

دالگ دز یا سینه خوه‌ی یا سینه کوتێ

The thief's mother either eats breast, or beats her chest

**Dengê le bini çaLaw tîyey**

ده‌نگێ له بن چاڵاو تییه‌ی

His voice comes from the bottom of the well
[Effete, Weak]

**DaLig bün u düyet bixwaz - Ta nekefye neng u waz**

دالگ بۆن و دۆیه‌ت بخواز ـ تا نه‌که‌فیه نه‌نگ و واز

Look at the mother and marry the daughter - so you may avoid problem and shame

**DaL pîr bû, kûrkûrek tülekî we pê keyd**

دالٚ پیر بوو، کوورکوورهک تۆله‌کی وه پێ که‌ید

When the vulture becomes old it gets ridiculed by the moth

**Darig heres bûd, ras çûde ban**

دارگ هه‌رس بوود، راس چووده بان

A pruned tree, grows straight

**Darê ki saLê berr negrê, nîyewirrnê**

دارێ ک سالێ به‌ر نه‌گرێ، نییه‌ورنێ

A tree that does not bear fruit one year is not cut down

**Darê ki rrimê, bizan kefêde kam la(we)**

دارێ ک رمێ، بزان که‌فێده کام لا

When a tree falls, look which way it falls

**DaLig wisaye, daye le xwey çü**

دالگ وسایه، دایه له خوه‌ی چۆ

The mother is carefree, the wet-nurse worries to death

22

**Du kes biçne lay qazî - Yekê tîyeydew we razî**

دو کەس بچنە لای قازی ـ یەکێ تییەیدەو وە رازی

When two people go to the judge, only one of them returns happy

**Dûs desê bişkin, desxirrey meke**

دووس دەسێ بشکن، دەسخڕەی مەکە

Break your friend's arm, but do not betray him

**Du gêa (gida) le seri maL dewLemenê bîye cengîyan**

دو گنیا (گدا) لە سەر ماڵ دەوڵەمەنێ بییە جەنگییان

Two beggars fought in front of the rich man's house

**Düyay tirrîn qing sift girtine**

دۆیای تڕین قنگ سفت گرتنە

After farting, you keep tight

**Desi zûr saman neyrê**

دەس زوور سامان نەیرێ

No good comes out of the hand of power

**Des kar keyd, çew tersê**

دەس کار کەید، چەو تەرسێ

The hand does its, the eyes fear

**Desim bişkê negi pam - Bawem bimrê negi dam**

دەسم بشکێ نەگ پام ـ باوەم بمرێ نەگ دام

May my arm be broken, not my leg - May my father die, not my mother

**Desi merdim mar we pê girin**

دەس مەردم مار وە پێ گرن

Capture a snake with people's hands

**Des nerm u nazik, derzî pûLadîn**

دەس نەرم و نازک، دەرزی پوولادین

Soft and smooth hands, needle of steel

[Those who accept something even though they know that it does not lead to anything good]


**Desê ki qanûn bûridê, xünê nîyetê(nîyetyê)**

دەسێ ک قانوون بووریدێ، خۆنێ نییەتێ

The hand cut by the law, does not bleed

[The state does not pay for bloodshed]


**Desê ki natwanî bûrîdê, maçi bike**

دەسێ ک ناتوانی بووریدێ، ماچێ بکه

If you can not cut off the hand, kiss it


**Demi sey we tike bûwes**

دەم سەی وه تکه بووس

Shut the dog's mouth with a piece of meat


**Demi merdim qingi min nîye ta bigirmey**

دەم مەردم قنگ من نییه تا بگرمەی

Peoples mouth is not my ass for me to keep tight


**Demê dûşawe, diLê zûxawe**

دەمێ دووشاوه، دلێ زۆخاوه

The old man's mouth is like syrup, his heart is full of sorrow/pus


**Deyig hes xa keyd, deyig hes xa xweyd**

دەیگ هەس خا کەید، دەیگ هەس خا خوەید

One village 'manufactures' eggs, the other village eats eggs

**Dîni hini dînare**

دین هن دیناره

Money is his religion


**DêwiL dirryêd, beLm kene tê**

دێوڵ دریێد، بهڵم کهنهتێ

When the drum breaks, they fill it with straw


# E

**Eger gurg neüd (nêd), segeyl (segel) xwened**

ئهگهر گورگ نهۆد، سهگهیل خوهنهد

Had it not been for the wolf, one had been eaten by the dogs


**Eger hîçî nîyezanî - gûçan heLgir eray şûwanî**

ئهگهر هیچی نییهزانی ـ گووچان ههڵگر ئهرای شووانی

If you don't know anything - Take a stick and become a shepherd


**Eger Îsa new; Eger Mûsa new; Xuda xudadarî xwey keyd**

ئهگهر ئیسا نهو؛ ئهگهر مووسا نهو؛ خودا خوداداری خوهی کهید

Had not Jesus or Moses existed, God would continue to be God (do what God does)


**Eger le çeqeL bitirsyam, mamir nîyenyamew**

ئهگهر له چهقهڵ بترسیام، مامر نییهنیامهو

If I were afraid of the jackal, I had not bred chickens

**Eger sûwar u pa pîya bitwan des bikene mil yek, yey mil çemnêd ew pa hîz deyd**

ئەگەر سووار و پا پیا بتوان دەس بکەنە مل یەک، یەی مل چەمنێد ئەو پا هیز دەید

If the rider and the pedestrian are to hug, one has to bend and the other has to rise

**Eger tu dizzî, tîyerîke-şew fires [Er terye xasigid, tîyerîkî şew fires]**

ئەگەر تو دزی، تییەریکەشەو فرەس

If you are a thief, there is plenty of darkness at night

**Eger zûwan bîlê, ser seLamete**

ئەگەر زووان بیلێ، سەر سەڵامەتە

If the tongue would allow, the head is well

**EqLê ha çewê**

ئەقلێ ها چەوێ

He believes in what he sees

**Erwawî êwaran miziney bigir, eşxaL şewekyan**

ئەرواوی ئێواران مزنەی بگر، ئەشخاڵ شەوەکیان

Cultivate the land in the afternoon; take care of the cattle in the morning

**Elan ki taLan taLane - setmenî ( sed tumenî) jêri paLane**

ئەلان ک تاڵان تاڵانە سەتمەنی ( سەد تومەنی) ژێر پاڵانە

Now that there is looting and plunder, the money is under the saddle

**Er bawgit nedîgîm le xusey daLigit mirdîm**

ئەر باوگت نەدیگیم لە خوسەی داڵگت مردیم

Had I not seen your father, I would have died because of your mother

**Er bedgû neü(w), mîye u gurg de yey ca aw xwen**

ئەر بەدگوو نەۆ، مییە و گورگ دە یەی جا ئاو خوەن

If there was no hypocrite, the sheep and the wolf would drink from the same river

**Er bizanisam kam rûj me mirdim, laney awadanim derwes mekirdim**

ئەر بزانسام کام ڕووژ مە مردم، لانەی ئاوادانم دەروەس مەکردم

Had I known when I die, I would have closed my house!

**Er dîrî dirêxt neke, er neyrî qert neke**

ئەر دیری درێخت نەکە، ئەر نەیری قەرت نەکە

If you have (money), waste no time - If you don't have, do not borrow

**Er dît ezim - er neyt dizim**

ئەر دیت ئەزم - ئەر نەیت دزم

If you saw me, it was I - If you did not see me, I am the thief

**Er guL nîyid, we dirrig mew**

ئەر گوڵ نیید، وە درگ مەو

If you are not a flower, do not stick us with your thorns

**Er keLeşêr nequLnê, dî rûj nîyew?**

ئەر کەلەشێر نەقولنێ، دی ڕووژ نییەو؟

If the rooster did not crow, would it not be a new day?

**Er kur xasige, werr xwey de aw dirarê**

ئەر کوڕ خاسگە، وەڕ خوەی دە ئاو درارێ

If he is such a good boy, let him extract his own 'coat' out of the river

27

**Er sürim kirdî wene (weger ne) xawmaw bird!**

ئەر سۆرم کردی وەنە خاوماو برد!

Either marry me or I am not interested


**Er tu fikrê dîrî, me fikr u nîmê dîrim!**

ئەر تو فکری دیری، مه فکر و نیمی دیرم!

If you have an idea, I have one and a half


**Er tu neüşî kûrî, xwem nîyezanim taney ha çewim? [Tu neüşe pêm kûrî, xwem zanim taneyg ha le çewim]**

ئەر تو نەۆشی کووری، خوەم نییەزانم تانەی ها چەوم؟

If you hadn't told me I have a dot in my eye (Blind) don't you think I would know it myself?


**Er tu yey minî, me sed minim**

ئەر تو یەی منی، مه سەد منم

If you are one of me, I am hundreds of me


**Er tûway mar negrêded, le küye la we la biçû**

ئەر تووای مار نەگرێدەد، له کۆیه لا وه لا بچوو

If you don't want to be bitten by a snake, walk sideways up the mountain


**Er we temaşa büde usa, seg îse qesaw bü**

ئەر وه تەماشا بۆده ئوسا، سەگ ئیسه قەساو بۆ

If one could be an expert by watching, the dog had been a butcher by now


**Er xwazî ezîz bûy, ya bimrî ya dür bûy!**

ئەر خوازی ئەزیز بووی، یا بمری یا دۆر بووی!

If you want to be held dear by the people, you should either be dead or far away

**Er xwere, wey we keçeL - Er warane, wey we keçeL**

ئەر خوەرە، وەی وە کەچەڵ ـ ئەر وارانە، وەی وە کەچەڵ

If it's sunny, pity the bald. If it's rainy, pity the bald

**Era merdim zerrim - Era xwem şerrim**

ئەرا مەردم زەرم ـ ئەرا خوەم شەرم

For others, I'm gold - For myself I'm trouble

**Era temam merdim daye! Era îme bawejin!**

ئەرا تەمام مەردم دایە! ئەرا ئیمە باوەژن!

Calls the people dear mother! Calls us stepmother!

**Era ye üşimet kake, melüçigi eram bûwerşnî**

ئەرا یە ئۆشمەت کاکە، مەلۆچگ ئەرام بووەرشنی

The reason I call you sir, is, so you grill me a sparrow

**Eray danüke tek deyde werew, eray xage çûde cay tirek**

ئەرای دانۆکه تەک دەیده وەرەو، ئەرای خاگه چووده جای ترەک

You are first in line for the seeds, when you lay eggs you hide

**Erê kesi bimir, tew erad bikey [Eray kesê tew bike, erad bimrê]**

ئەرێ کەسێ بمر، تەو ئەراد بکەی

Die for the one that makes you feverish

**Erzan nesen girane, giran bisen erzane**

ئەرزان نەسەن گرانە، گران بسەن ئەرزانە

Do not buy cheap for it's expensive, buy expensive for it's cheap
[Quality]

**Esp le cay nerm ayim rrimnê, xer le cay sext**

ئەسپ لە جای نەرم ئایم رمنێ، خەر لە جای سەخت

A horse throws you off in soft soil, a donkey in hard

**Espi xwed miyenê meke**

ئەسپ خوەد میەنێ مەکە

Do not wear down your own horse

**Ewqere baw u biçû, qurbid neçû**

ئەوقەرە باو و بچوو، قوربد نەچوو

Come and go as you please, just make sure people do not lose their respect for you

**Espi bidew, dani zîyay keyd**

ئەسپێ بدەو، دانێ زییای کەید

Increase the fodder for the fast steed

**ELeng eLeng le çingi şêr derçîm, keftime çingi peLeng**

ئەڵەنگ ئەڵەنگ لە چنگ شیر دەرچیم، کەفتمە چنگ پەڵەنگ

I narrowly escaped the lion's claws, to end up in the leopard's claws

[Between a rock and a hard place]

**Encîri merdim ew desid nîyerisê, we dûşaw (dîşaw) xwed bijye**

ئەنجیر مەردم ئەو دەسد نییەرسێ، وە دووشاو خوەد بژیە

You can not catch people's fig, live of your own syrup

**Engür (enür) er engür nûrê, aw heLgirê**

ئەنگۆر ئەر ئەنگۆر نوورێ، ئاو ھەڵگرێ

When the grape looks at the grape, it matures

**Ewri wehar we yey lawa warêd**

ئەور وەھار وە یەی لاوا وارێد

Spring clouds rain suddenly

**Ew mare ki tu rixid lê çû, me serê tilanime**

ئەو مارە ک تو رخد لێ چوو، مە سەرێ تلانمە

I smashed the head of the snake you were afraid of

**EweL pîyaLe u bed mesî?**

ئەوەڵ پییاڵە و بەد مەسی؟

First glass/shot and already drunk?

[Big talk]

**Ewey ki gîrêd yê derd dîrê, ewey ki xenêd hizar u yê derd**

ئەوەی ک گیرێد یێ دەرد دیرێ، ئەوەی ک خەنێد ھزار و یێ دەرد

The crying one has a problem, the laughing one has a thousand and one problems

**Er yewaş rê kem şerr resêde pêma – Er tin rê kem resime şerrew**

ئەر یەواش رێ کەم شەڕ رەسێدە پێما – ئەر تن رێ کەم رەسمە شەڕەو

If I walk slowly, the problems catch up with me – If I walk fast, I catch up with the problems

# Ê

**Êware bixef, axir dinyas – Şewekî eLis, eweL dinyas**

ئێواره بخەف، ئاخر دنیاس – شەوەکی ئەلَس، ئەوەلَ دنیاس

Sleep at night, it is the end of time- Wake up in the morning, it is the beginning of time

# F

**FiLanî gemaLê daşt, meresê besa milê, çirrîyê: Tancî, tancî**

فلَانی گەمالَی داشت، مەرەسی بەسا ملنی، چڕیینی: تانجی، تانجی

The old man had an old dog, he put a necklace around its neck and cried: hunting dog, hunting dog (Greyhound)

**Fêrege fêrê meke – Eger kirdî têrê bike**

فێرەگە فێرێ مەکە– ئەگەر کردی تێری بکه

Don't teach the wise anything – If you do, make sure to satisfy him

# G

**Ga bar kuşêdey, merd (pîya ) hamaL**

گا بار کوشێدەی، مەرد هامالَ

Burden kills the bull, competition kills the man

**Ga le gûrî dîyare**

گا لەگوورى دییاره

By looking at the calf you know how the bull will be

**Ga mird u şîre u yere birrya**

گا مرد و شیره و یهره بریا

The cow died and the cooperative was disbanded (see: şîre u yere )

**Ga mirê kîyerd fire bû**

گا مرئ کییهرد فره بوو

When the cow dies there will be plenty of daggers

**Gawan le gawanî arê nat – Le nan cema kirdin arê hat**

گاوان له گاوانی ئارئ نات – له نان جهما کردن ئارئ هات

The cowherd was not ashamed for being a cowherd – He was ashamed for being forced to collect bread (fodder for his cows)

**Ga we bûrrewa nasêd**

گا وه بوورهوا ناسئد

One recognizes the cow from its cry

**Ga we demi ciftyar nûrrê**

گا وه دهم جفتیار نوورئ

The cow looks at the farmer's mouth!
[Anyone who takes the ideas of others and makes it his own]

**Gayg eray camig dû êwet nîyeken**

گایگ ئهرای جامگ دوو ئێوهت نییهکهن

No one breeds a cow for a glass of yoghurt drink

**Gayg hate mêze mêze, axirê mêze**

گایگ هاته مێزهمێزه، ئاخرئ مێزه

A cow who has to relieve itself, will relieve itself!
[If you have to then you have to]

33

**Giryêg we des waz bû, era we dêan (digan) wazê keyd?**

گرێگ وه دەس واز بوو، ئەرا وه دێئان وازێ کەید؟

Why use teeth on a knot that can be untied with your hands?

**Gurg çüzanê qîmeti qatir çene**

گورگ چۆزانێ قیمەت قاتر چەنه

What does the wolf know how much a donkey is worth!

**Gurg girtinê mixtê bîyen, wet: Wilim ken rîyen der çî**

گورگ گرتنێ مختێ بییەن، وەت: ولم کەن رییەن دەر چی

They caught the wolf to give it a beating, the wolf said: Let me go, the pack gets away

**Gurg le wexti tengî pişt kenew yek**

گورگ له وەخت تەنگی پشت کەنەو یەک

Wolves are united in the hour of danger

**Gurg nawê beyd, hazire [Naw gurg beyd, hazire]**

گورگ ناوێ بەید، هازره

If you mention the wolf's name, it's ready!

**Gurg hegi pîr bû, bûdine rîşq(x)enî seg**

گورگ هەگێ پیر بوو، بوودنه ریشقەنی سەگ

When the wolf grows old, it becomes ridiculed by the dogs

**Gûşt hersey girane, nexwardinî erzane**

گووشت هەرسەی گرانه، نەخواردنی ئەرزانه

When the meat is expensive, it is cheap not to eat it

**Gûşti yek buxwen, siqan yek nîyeşkinin**

گووشت یەک بوخوەن، سقان یەک نییەشکنن

Hurt each other, but do not break each other's bones

34

## Gûşti heLaLe, awgûşti herame
گووشتی هەڵاڵە، ئاوگووشتی هەرامە
His meat is halal (lawful), his stew is haram (unlawful)

## GemaL ew le Bexda tirrê, nani me leyra ( le îra ) bûde cüye
گەمێڵ ئەو لە بەخدا تڕێ، نان مە لەیرا بووده جۆیه
The old dog (Wali of pusht-i-kuh) farts in Baghdad, over here my bread turns to rye

## GemaL qulê şikê, düyê besin [Sey qulê şikê düyê girinew]
گەمێڵ قولی شکێ، دۆیی بەسن
The old dog broke its leg, they plaster casted its tail

## Geni xwem le xasi merdim xastire
گەن خوەم لە خاس مەردم خاسترە
My worst is better than people's best

## Gêa (Gida) er yekê bû, gayg eray ser birrin
گێیا ئەر یەکێ بوو، گایگ ئەرای سەر بڕن
If the beggars had been one, they would have slaughtered a cow for him

## Gêa rüyê reşe u türegey pirre
گێیا ڕۆیی ڕەشه و تۆرمگەی پڕه
The beggar has a dirty face and a full sack

## Gîyan çûde cayg, kirm u mûr xweydey
گییان چووده جایگ، کرم و موور خوەیدەی
The soul rests in a place where it is eaten by worms and ants

**Gîya we cî sextew mînê**

گییا وه جی سهختهو مینئ

The plant remains, in inaccessible places!

**Gîweker pay petîye**

گیوهکهر پای پهتییه

The shoemaker is barefoot

**Girrme hirr bûwari, baran newari**

گرمهھر بوواری، باران نهواری

May it flash and thunder, as long as it doesn't rain
[About wrath]

**Gîwe kûwane le bîyaban nêmete**

گیوه کووانه له بییابان نێمهته

Worn shoes are invaluable in the desert

**GuL pişt u rü nêri**

گوڵ پشت و رۆ نێرئ

Flowers lack front and back side

**Gunakar derçü le tafi dew - bîguna girya le şesi xew**

گوناکار دهر چۆ له تافئ دهو ـ بیگونا گریا له شهسئ خهو

The culprit got away because of his speed - the innocent
got caught because of his doziness

**Gûz werawer gûz, xurma binerxi rûj [Gûz we nirxi gûz –
Xurma we nirxi rûj]**

گووز وهراوهر گووز، خورما بنهرخئ رووژ

Bullshit equivalent to bullshit, date equivalent to today's
price

**Gunakar minakar [Minakar, gunakar]**

گوناکار مناکار

A sinner is the one who prohibits others

# H

**HeLaLxwerî le kemdesîye**

هەڵاڵخوەری لە کەمدەسییه

Honest living is due to poverty / weakness

**Her ke we rê xwey**

هەر کە وە ڕێ خوەی

Each his own way

**Hemam we pif germew nîyew**

هەمام وە پف گەرمەو نییەو

The bath is not heated with a fart

**Her guLê bûwig dîri**

هەر گوڵێ بووگ دیرێ

Each flower has its own smell

**Heya tikêge; (Er) tikya, şermê nîyemînêd**

هەیا تکێگە؛ (ئەر) تکیا، شەرمێ نییەمینێد

Shame is a drop; If it drops, there is nothing left!

**Heq bizini hil we lay bizini şaxdar nîyemênê**

هەق بزن هل وە لای بزن شاخدار نییەمینێ

The hornless goat's right remains not with the horned goat

**Hec ha deri maL xwed**

هەج ها دەر ماڵ خوەد

Pilgrimage (hajj) is outside your own door

**Heyadar le heyay xwey tirsê; Bîheya üşê lêm tirsê**

هەیادار لە هەیای خوەی ترسێ؛ بی هەیا ئۆشێ لێم ترسێ

A respectable person fears his shamelessness; The shameless says: He fears me

**Heywaneyl le xişe wan, gurg tek deyde wer**

هەیوانەیل لە خشه وان، گورگ تەک دەیدە وەر

Animals flee the sound of rustle, the wolf walks up to it

**Ha seri kilig şeytanew**

ها سەر کلگ شەیتانەو

He is controlled by the devil

**HamaLî hem xaye tûway hem maye**

هاماڵی هەم خایه تووای هەم مایه

Competition requires both courage and capital

**Hizar dûs keme, yê dişmen fires**

هزار دووس کەمه، یێ دشمەن فرەس

A thousand friends are too few, one enemy is one too many

**Hüç kes maL bira beş nîyekey, bêcge birajin**

هۆچ کەس مال برا بەش نییەکەی، بێجگه براژن

No one gives away his brother's riches, except for the sister-in-law

**Hûkare (hukare) le gurg har bedtire**

هووکاره (هوکاره) لە گورگ هار بەدتره

The addict is worse than a rabid wolf

38

**Her çê heqe, wişk u reqe**

هەر چێ هەقه، وشک و ڕەقه

The truth is hard and dry

**Her çê ha le zatid, derîxê meke**

هەر چێ ها له زاتد، دەریخێ مەکه

Do not hesitate with what you have in mind

**Hersey zêw fires – Qewr we enazes**

هەرسەی زێو فرەس – قەور وه ئەنازس

Although there is plenty of land – The graves are made to measure

**Her ke tûrya, beşê xurya**

هەر که تووریا، بەشێ خوریا

The one who sulked (and went) had his share taken

**Her kes der kefê, wer kefê**

هەر کەس دەر کەفێ، وەر کەفێ

One who ends up outside, ends up in front!

**Her ke le maL çü, le ixtîyar çü**

هەر که له مالْ چۆ، له ئختییار چۆ

One who abandons his house, abandons his will

**Her ke we seng u meni xwey**

هەر که وه سەنگ و مەن خوەی

Each according to his prerequisite

**Her gûrê le gûreyl dür bû, wefir qulê birrê**

هەر گوورێ له گوورەیل دۆر بوو، وەفر قولێ بڕێ

The calf that alienates itself from other calves get its legs cut by the snow

**Her ke bişnewê deng u dawiman – Dî bari nîyetyerê erê asîyawiman**

هەر کە بشنەوێ دەنگ و داومان — دی بار نییەتیەرێ وە ئاسییاوومان

If anyone would hear our fights - nobody would fetch their cargo to our mill

**Her melê zewaL melêge**

هەر مەلێ زەوالَ مەلێگە

Each creature is another's burden

**Hegi tengide we misewî daLigid büş kake**

هەمگێ تەنگدە وە مسەوی دالَگد بۆش کاکە

When you are in dire need, call your mother's boyfriend Sir

**HeLperge nîyezanê, üşê: Hisaregedan çefte!**

هەلَپەرگە نییەزانێ، ئۆشێ: هسارەگەدان چەفتە!

He can not dance and excuses himself by saying: Your yard leans

**HeLmetê le mîyetê xastire**

هەلَمەتێ لە مییەتێ خاسترە

His attack is better than his help

**Hem xuda tûway hem xurma**

هەم خودا تووای هەم خورما

Wants both God and date
[Eat the cake and keep it]

40

**Hemey maLegem kutê qalîye – Bixemey ewla, îlay xalîye**

هەمەی مالْەگەم کوتیٔ قالییە۔ بخەمەی ئەولا، ئیلای خالییە

My entire wealth is a carpet – If I spread it here, it will be empty there

**Hîç kam-man le hîç kam-man negrîm tawan – Yekê bûde luwîne, yekê we gawan**

هیچ کاممان لە هیچ کاممان نەگریم تاوان – یەکیٔ بوودە لووینە، یەکیٔ وە گاوان

Let us not blame each other - One becomes a Miller, and one becomes a cowherd

# Ii

**Imrû le mine, sûwa le tine**

ئمروو لە منە، سووا لە تنە

Today I'll pay, tomorrow you'll pay

# Î

**Î mirîje, rêy dirîje**

ئی مریژە، رێی دریژە

This ant has a long way to go

**Î xere new xerêtir – PaLanê kem we rengêtir**

ئی خەرە نەو خەرینتر – پالْانیٔ کەم وە رەنگینتر

If not this donkey, then another - I will make a saddle in a different colour

**Î dese we cî ew desege nîyewirrin**

ئی دەسە وە جی ئەو دەسەگە نییەورن

One does not cut a hand instead of another

**Î rawe eray rûwîye**

ئی راوە ئەرای رووییە

This hunt is for the Fox

**Îra new îratir – Î kene new, kenêtir**

ئیرا نەو ئیراتر – ئی کەنە نەو، کەنێتر

If it is not possible here then somewhere else – If not this spring then another

# J

**Jijû üşê: Le minaLi me nermtir kî dîye?**

ژژوو ئۆشێ: لە منالٚ مە نەرمتر کی دییە؟

The hedgehog says: Are there any child softer than mine?

**Jin bennase, mêre karger**

ژن بەننٚاسە، مێرە کارگەر

Woman is the architect, man her laborer

**Jini bî şü, kemçigi bî dü**

ژن بی شۆ، کەمچگێ بی دۆ

Unmarried woman, handleless ladle

**Jinê xêz bixerey çem, dawanê terr nîyew**

ژنێ خێز بخەرەی چەم، داوانێ تەر نییەو

If you throw a wise woman into the river, she will come out dry

**Jin le müş tirsê,müş le pişî, pişî le sey, sey le pîya u pîya le jin**

ژن له مۆش ترسێ،مۆش له پشی، پشی له سهی، سهی له پییا و پییا له ژن

Women fear mice, mice fear cats, cats fear dogs, dogs fear men, and men fear women

**Jin nîyeçûde pişti bira – Çûde pişti şü**

ژن نییهچوو ده پشت برا – چووده پشت شۆ

The woman does not support her brother - She supports her husband

# K

**Kase erê kû eçê, we şûn kuçLe**

کاسه ئهرێ کوو ئهچێ، وه شوون کوچله

Where does the turtle go, to the stones!

**Kem buxwe, hemîşe buxwe [Kem bixwe, dayim bixwe]**

کهم بوخوه، ههمیشه بوخوه

Eat a little, eat always

**Kemçig dü dêri**

کهمچگ دۆ دێرێ

The ladle has tail

**Kuçig eger seyînî, paL bê pîyew**

کوچگ ئهگهر سهیینی، پاڵ بێ پییهو

If the stone is too heavy, push harder

**Kuçig le şûn xwey seyîne [San le cay xwey seyîne]**

کوچگ له شوون خوهی سهیینه

The stone is secure in its place

**Kûzeçî le kûze şikyag aw exwa**

کووزەچی لە کووزە شکیاگ ئاو ئەخوا

The potter drinks from a broken pot


**Kari gen meke u le xuda meLaLikye**

کار گەن مەکە و لە خودا مەڵاڵکیە

Do not commit sin and fear (beseech) not God


**Kasêg beşi me tê newd, demi bûde xwar**

کاسێگ بەش مە تێ نەود، دەمێ بووده خوار

Let the bowl I have no part in, be upside down


**Kasêg ki kêwanû bişiknidê, dengi nîyetê**

کاسێگ ک کێوانوو بشکندێ، دەنگێ نییەتێ

The bowl broken by the (old) woman does not make a sound


**Kuçig ew hüri diz mexe**

کوچگ ئەو هۆر دز مەخە

Don't remind the thief of stones


**Kûr ta mirê (emrê) we temay çewe**

کوور تا مرێ وە تەمای چەوە

Until the moment of death the blind wishes sight


**Kûre xweşe? Ewre ki diL xweşe!**

کووره خوەشە؟ ئەوره ک دڵ خوەشە!

Where is home? Anywhere you are happy


**Kul darê guL keyd weLam berr nîyegrêd**

کول دارێ گوڵ کەید وەڵام بەر نییەگرێد

All trees bloom but not all of them bear fruit

**Kul melê gûştxwere, gurg bed nawe**

کول مەڵێ گووشتخۆرە، گورگ بەد ناوه

All predators are carnivores, only the wolf has a bad reputation


**Ker du car xenêd**

کەر دو جار خەنێد

The deaf laughs twice


**Kes we dû xwey nîyeüşê (nayjê) tirş**

کەس وه دوو خۆەی نییەوشێ ترش

No one calls his own yogurt sour


**Kesê keL kuşê, bawgi keL kuştü**

کەسێ کەڵ کۆشێ، باوگێ کەڵ کوشتو

One slays a ram whose father before him slew a ram


**Kesê mangay wişk êwet nîyekey**

کەسێ مانگای وشک ئێوەت نییەکەی

No one breeds a cow whose milk has dried up


**KeLên aw rişnê, büçig pay sirr bey**

کەڵێن ئاو رشنێ، بۆچگ پای سر بەی

The mighty pours water, the weak slips


**Kem-beş büd, bê-beş neüd**

کەم بەش بۆد، بێ بەش نەۆد

Rather a small share than no share at all


**Key le xwed neü, kêan le xwed bü**

کەی له خۆەد نەۆ، کنیان له خۆەد بۆ

If the hay isn't yours, make sure the hayshed is

**Kîyerdi jîri werr**

کییەردێ ژیرێ وەڕ

The dagger beneath the coat

[He who hates and wants to harm someone but do not
get the opportunity]

**Kîyerdi jîri werr; Ya werr dirrê, ya zig xawini werr**

کییەردێ ژیرێ وەڕ؛ یا وەڕ دڕێ، یا زگ خاونێ وەڕ

The dagger beneath the coat; Either cuts the coat, or its
owner's stomach

**Kuçig exade nûway diz**

کوچگ ئەخادە نووای دز

Throws rock in front of the thief

[Warns]

# L

**Le nûkase [Nûkîse] qert neke - eger qert kirdî, xerci neke**

لە نووکاسە قەرت نەکە ئەگەر قەرت کردی، خەرجێ نەکە

Do not borrow from the newly rich – If you borrow, do
not spend it

**Le qatir pirsîn kî bawgide? Wet esp xaLûme!**

لە قاتر پرسین کی باوگدە؟ وەت ئەسپ خاڵوومە!

They asked the mule who his father is? The mule said:
Horse is my uncle

[Ashamed of his origin]

**Laf herçê küyenetire (kûwanetire), aLûşê fêştire**

لاف هەرچێ کۆیەنەترە،ئاڵووشێ فێشترە

The older a blanket, the more it itches

**Laney mûrî (mirüj) we şewnimê wêrane**

لانەی موورى وه شەونمێ وێرانه

An ant's house gets devastated by a drop

**Luqmey qeü hem dem dirrêd hem qing dirrêd**

لوقمەی قەۆ هەم دەم درێد هەم قنگ درێد

A big bite ruptures both mouth and ass

**Le agir xuLekû kefêdew**

له ئاگر خولەکوو کەفێدەو

Ashes fall of the fire

**Le cüye direw bike ta newbey genim tîyê**

له جۆیە درەو بکه تا نەوبەی گەنم تییێ

Harvest the rye until it's time for the wheat

**Le çingi heLing derçü, kefte çingi peLing**

له چنگ هەڵنگ دەرچۆ، کەفته چنگ پەڵنگ

He fled the vulture's claws to end up in the leopard's claws

**Le dûzex bijyey we azad, ne le beheyşt bijyey we newker**

له دووزەخ بژیەی وه ئازاد، نه له بەهەیشت بژیەی وه نەوکەر

Rather free in hell than slave in paradise

**Le jini şelîte u segi har bitirs**

له ژن شەلیته و سەگ هار بترس

Fear a shameless woman and a rabid dog

**Le rîşi birrê deyde sêwiLê**

له ریشێ برێ دەیده سێوڵێ

He cuts off his beard and gives it to his moustache

**Le zimsan kunayg çene çew gayig, çene leş gayig serma kîşê**

له زمسان کونایگ چەنە چەو گایگ، چەنە لەش گایگ سەرما کیشێ

In winter, a hole as big as a bull's eye, cools down as much as a bull's body


**Le kul ewrê nîyewarê**

لە کول ئەورێ نییەوارێ

Not every cloud has rain


**Le kîsey xelîfe bexşê**

لە کیسەی خەلیفە بەخشێ

He bestows from the emperor's coffin


**Lewre tengime, resinim kefêde girye (gire)**

لەورە تەنگمە، رەسنم کەفێدە گریە

Wherever I have a problem, there my rope tangles


# M

**MaLid eger le şîşes, kuçig mexe le hewsa**

مالد ئەگەر لە شیشەس، کوچگ مەخە لە هەوسا

If your house is made of glass, do not throw stones at the neighbour's house


**Mar bedi le pünge hat, pünge çü le der kunagey sewz bî**

مار بەدێ لە پۆنگە هات، پۆنگە چۆ لە دەر کوناگەی سەوز بی

The snake disliked mint; mint grew at its burrow!


**Margezyag le ben sîye we çermig rixi eçi**

مارگەزیاگ لە بەن سییە وە چەرمگ رخێ ئەچێ

One bitten by a snake, fears black and white ropes


48

**Melîçig buxwe, mecükin**

مەلیچگ بوخوه، مەجۆکن

Little bird eat and do not cackle

**Miymûn netwanist bireqsi, wet zêwege çefte**

میموون نەتوانست برەقسێ، وەت زێوەگە چەفتە

The monkey could not dance, it said: the ground is leaning

**Me üşim aw nîye, ew üşê bikerey lîtige**

مە ئۆشم ئاو نییە، ئەو ئۆشێ بکەرەی لیتگە

I say there is no water, he says make me some soup

**Me üşim nêre, ew üşê bûşey**

مە ئۆشم نێرە، ئەو ئۆشێ بووشەی

I say it is a male, he says milk it

**Mar guna keyd, tawanê marmülig deyd**

مار گونا کەید، تاوانێ مارمۆلگ دەید

The serpent sins, the lizard gets the blame

**Mar mar xwey**

مار مار خوەی

Snake eats snake

**Mar herçê pêç xwey, ras çûde kunawa**

مار هەرچێ پێچ خوەی، راس چووده کوناوا

It doesn't matter how much the snake coils itself, when it enters it's lair, it is straight

**MaL-birryay le birayş ha şek**

مالْبرریای لە برایش ها شەک

A robbed person suspects his own brother

49

**MaLi xwey pê bifrûş**

مالَ خوەی پێ بفرووش

Sell him his own property

**MaLi di (du) kêwanû – Xakê tîyey ta zanû**

مالَ د کێوانوو – خاکێ تییەی تا زانوو

The dust in two old woman's house reaches the knees

**MaLi dinya tîyeyda, bira nîyetîyeyda!**

مالَ دنیا تییەیدا، برا نییەتییەیدا!

The worldly things returns, your brother will not

**MaL le deri kunay mar sazê**

مالَ له دەر کونای مار سازێ

Builds his house in front of the snake's lair

**MaL we mêmanew xweşe**

مالَ وه مێمانەو خوەشه

A nice home is a home filled with guests

**Mamir aw xwey rü le xuda keyd**

مامر ئاو خوەی رۆ له خودا کەید

When the hen drinks, it looks up to God

**Manga we dizîyew keL girê we aşkira zayid**

مانگا وه دزییەو کەلَ گرێ وه ئاشکرا زاید

The cow mates in secret, gives birth openly

**Mang we çew düniney, we kilig işarey ken**

مانگ وه چەو دۆننەی، وه کلگ نشارەی کەن

One sees the moon with the naked eye, pointing at it with a finger!

50

**Me çe müşim, sazim çe mejenê**

مه چه مۆشم، سازم چه مەژەنێ

What am I saying, what is my flute singing?

**Me xan u tu xan, kî hewLege biranê?**

مه خان و تو خان، کی هەولێگه برانێ؟

I king and you king, who will drive the load?

**Mirdê u zinê we aw pakew bûn**

مردێ و زنێ وه ئاو پاکەو بوون

The dead and the living are cleaned with water

**MinaL ta negîrê, memig we demê nîyenen (nanen)**

منآل تا نەگیرێ، مەمگ وه دەمێ نییەنەن

So long the infant does not cry, it will not get any milk

**MinaL nû-pa, nû (nüye) nefer le pa xeyd**

منآل نووپا، نوو نەفەر له پا خەید

A child who just learned to walk, fatigues nine people

**Merd şü neyrê, qert şüye**

مەرد شۆ نەیرێ، قەرت شۆیه

A man has no husband, loan is his spouse

**Meke, le sewr betire (bedtire)**

مەکه، له سەور بەتره

Not being allowed to do is worse than patience

**Mîrati xerr, hini kemtare**

میراتێ خەر، هن کەمتاره

The donkey is inherited by the hyena

**Mêman xweşê we mêman nat, xawin-maL we herdigî**

مێمان خوەشێ وە مێمان نات، خاوەنماڵ وە هەردگی

The guest disliked the guest, the host disliked them both

**Mîwe le şîrînî xwey, kirm deyde tê**

میوه له شیرینی خوەی، کرم دەیده تێ

A fruit is worm-eaten because of its own sweetness

# N

**Nan eray nanewa, gûşt eray qesaw**

نان ئەرای نانەوا، گووشت ئەرای قەساو

Bread for the baker, meat for the butcher

**Nanxwerê sifredirr**

نانخوەرێ سفرەدر

Eats his food and destroys the table

[Ungratefulness]

**Nicaset çû beyde lê, bûy bedtir bû**

نجاسەت چوو بەیدەلێ، بووی بەدتر بوو

If you stir the faeces, it will smell worse

**Nûrr (Nûwirr) du ser dîrê**

نوور دو سەر دیرێ

Curse is the two-headed

[A curse is like a two-edged sword]

**Ne ewqere şîrîn bû, qütid ben – Ne ewqere tîyeL bû, tifid biken**

نه ئەوقەره شیرین بوو، قۆتد بەن — نه ئەوقەره تییەڵ بوو، تفد بکەن

Don't be too sweet so they don't eat you – Don't be too bitter so they don't spit you out

**Nezan  çü zanê – Bizan çe zanê**

نەزان چۆ زانێ – بزان چە زانێ

Do not bother with HOW he knows, worry about WHAT he knows

**Ne zûwanê şîrîne – Ne gîrfanê sengîne**

نە زووانێ شیرینە– نە گیرفانێ سەنگینە

He has neither a smooth tongue, nor full pockets

**Ne derzîye bişikyê, ne meçîre bûwiryê**

نە دەرزییە بشکیێ، نە مەچیرە بوورییێ

He is neither a needle so he breaks, nor a thread so he snaps

**Ne maLim hes, rehman bûwey – Ne dînim hes şeytan bûwey**

نە مالّم هەس، رەهمان بووەی – نە دینم هەس شەیتان بووەی

I own nothing so the creator can take it from me - I own no faith so the devil can take it from me

**Ne we zûre u ne we herbey ney – Her kesê xwey we çarenüsi xwey**

نە وە زوورە و نە وە هەربەی نەی – هەر کەسێ خوەی وە چارەنۆس خوەی

It is neither by force nor by beating - Everyone his own destiny

**Nîyezanim u nîyetwanim, deway derde**

نییەزانم و نییەتوانم، دەوای دەردە

Don't know and can't are the best cures for headache

# P

**Pa çîye pacînge**

پا چییه پاجینگه

The foot was put in the climbing holes

**Padarege bigir, bîpage we cas (Padar bigir bîpa wil ke)**

پادارەگه بگر، بییاگه وه جاس

Take hold of the moving, the standing remains

**Pay mîye lerrew bû, Pay weren qeünew bû**

پای مییه لەرەو بوو، پای وەرەن قەۆنەو بوو

If the ewe's leg meagre, the ram's leg will fatten

**Pül Bêe (bide) şeyx, le meçit (mescid) der bike**

پۆل بیه شەیخ، له مەچت (مەسجد/مزگەوت) دەر بکه

Give money to the imam, leave the mosque

**Pes(pez) u gurg le yê cû aw xwen**

پەس و گورگ له یێ جوو ئاو خوەن

Sheeps and wolfs drink from the same stream

**PeLi xweyan, we dengi xweyan**

پەڵ خوەیان، وه دەنگ خوەیان

Their cliff (stone), their voice

**Peletê (Peletig) we milew büye, xew (xaw) nemenîye**

پەلەتێ (پەلەتگ) وه ملەو بۆیه، خەو نەمەنییه

The one who had a rope around his neck, had no sleep

**Penê ki we erzan le des bîyeydê, we giran senîdi**

پەنێ ک وه ئەرزان له دەس بییەیدێ، وه گران سەنیدێ

An advice lost easily, is bought costly

**Pîyagig ki pîyawetî daştû,le pîyenî asman pîyentire**

پییاگگ ک پییاوەتی داشتوو،لە پییەنی ئاسمان پییەنترە

A chivalrous man is wider than the width of the heaven

**Pîya we pile**

پییا وە پلە

Men based on category

**Pîran we tewê, zimsan we şewê**

پیران وە تەوئ، زمسان وە شەوئ

Old age with its fever, winter with its nights

**PêLa pişti pa gîre, düyet we pişti da gîre**

پێڵا پشت پا گیرە، دۆیەت وە پشت دا گیرە

The shoe is fixed to the heel; the daughter is fixed to her mother

**PîyeLman ha ew desi cû**

پییەڵمان ها ئەو دەس جوو

Our bridge is on the other side of the river

**Paşi le pêşi rey büye**

پاشئ لە پێشئ رەی بۆیە

His back has passed his front

[Confused]

# Q

**QeLa we qeLa eyjê rüd sîye [QiLa we qiLa üşê: Lay rüt sîyes]**

قەڵا وە قەڵا ئەیژئ رۆید سییە

The raven told the raven, your face is black

**Qewm eger mar bê, bîla hizar bê**

قەوم ئەگەر مار بێ، بیلا هزار بێ

If one's relatives are snakes, let them be in the thousands

**Qise tûki pîyaze**

قسه تووک پییازه

Talk is like the peels of an onion (Talk is cheap)

**Qise hizare, yekê le kare**

قسه هزاره، یەکێ له کاره

Of a thousand words, one is valid

**Qisey xweş le beheyştew hatîye**

قسەی خوش له بەهەیشتەو  هاتییه

Beautiful words are derived from paradise

**Qisey ras ya le minaL bişnew ya le şêt**

قسەی راس یا له منالْ بشنەو یا له شێت

You will hear the truth either from a child or a madman

**Qiseyg le bini sî u du dêan dirat, sî u du kes ejnewêdê**

قسەیگ له بن سی و دو دنیان درات، سی و دو کەس ئەژنەوێدێ

A sentence that passes through thirty-two teeth, is heard by thirty-two people

**QiLayg era yey şew sazin**

قلْایگ ئەرا یەی شەو سازن

They build a fort for a night

**Qert bike, jin bixwaz – Qertege deydew, jinege we cas**

قەرت بکە، ژن بخواز — قەرتەگە دەیدەو، ژنەگە وە جاس

Borrow money to marry - When you have paid off your loan, your wife remains!

**Qert şirrew bû, weLam nîyemirê**

قەرت شرەو بوو، وەڵام نییەمرێ

Loans become old but never die

**Qesaw le hewLi pîye – Bizin le hewLi pûs**

قەساو لە هەوڵی پییە— بزن لە هەوڵی پووس

The butcher worries about fat – The goat worries about its skin

**Qewr-ken bizanisya key mirê – Qewrig eray xwey kenyad**

قەورکەن بزانسیا کەی مرێ — قەورگ ئەرای خوەی کەنیاد

If the gravedigger knew when he would die - he would dig his own grave

# R

**Ras biçû, durus biçû**

ڕاس بچوو، دوروس بچوو

Go straight, go right

**Rûwa demi we enür nerisî, wet enüre turşe [Rûwî demê we encîr neresî wet kerres]**

ڕووا دەمێ وە ئەنۆر نەرسی، وەت ئەنۆرە تورشه

The fox could not reach the grape, it said: the grape is sour

**Rûwî we kunawa neçî, hejigê besa dü xweyew**

رووا وه کونا ناچی، دۆیێگ ئەرێ خوهییش وهسی

The fox didn't fit in the hole; it tied a branch to its tail

**Rûj we tep u tûz nîyeşaryeydew**

رووژ وه تەپ و تووز نییەشاریەیدەو

The day can not be hidden by dust

**Rûjê xeftim – Heft saL keftim**

رووژێ خەفتم – هەفت سالٚ کەفتم

I slept for one day - Lost seven years

**RûLe dî nemen dengi dilêran – Rûwî retinê le cagay şêran**

روولٚه دی نەمەن دەنگێ دلێران – رووی رەتنێ له جاگای شێران

My dear, there are no heroes left – The fox roars instead of the lion

**Rün firewe bû, qing we pê çewr ken**

رۆن فرەوه بوو، قنگ وه پێ چەور کەن

If there is plenty of oil, people will oil their asses with it

**Rûwî gurgê dî, heLperge le hürê çî**

رووی گورگێ دی، هەلٚپەرگه له هۆرێ چی

The fox saw the wolf and forgot how to dance

**Rûwî le maL xwey şêrige**

رووی له مالٚ خوهی شێرگه

The fox is a lion in its own house

**Resin birryey, çûwar ser pêa key**

رەسن بریەی، چووار سەر پێیا کەی

If you cut a rope, it will have four heads

**Rê diz yekêge, rê maL-xawin hizar**

رێ دز یەکێگە، رێ ماڵ-خاون هزار

The thief's path is one, the homeowner's path many

**Rîşi temakar ha qingi mufLis**

ریش تەماکار ها قنگ موفڵس

A greedy man's beard is stuck in the bankrupt's ass

**Refîqî sipLe u hamrahî gumra – Mekefe şûni kûr u naşareza**

رەفیقی سپڵه و هامراهی گومرا – مەکەفه شوون کوور و ناشارەزا

Friendship with a fool, and to go along with a lost one - Do not follow the blind and the ignorant

**Ras biçû we hakim meçû - Kem bixwe we hekîm meçû**

راس بچوو وه هاکم مەچوو - کەم بخوه وه هەکیم مەچوو

Be honest and avoid the judge – Eat moderately and avoid the doctor

**Ras cûr mü barîkew bûd, nîyewiryê**

راس جوور مۆ باریکەو بوود، نییەوریێ

If truth became as thin as a human hair, it would not snap

# S

**Saz we heway zemane jenê**

ساز وه هەوای زەمانه ژەنێ

The flute sings after the spirit of the times

**SaLi gen le weharê dîyare**

سالّی گەن لە وەهارئ دییارە

One recognizes a bad year by its spring

**SaL le nû, daL le nû**

سالّ لە نوو، دالّ لە نوو

New year, new place

**Sirrid lay yekê bine, pirsid lay hizar**

سرد لای یەکئ بنە، پرسد لای هزار

Tell your secret to one, your grief to thousands

**Sirke her çi tirş bû, zererê eray qapegey xweye**

سرکە هەر چ ترش بوو، زەرەرئ ئەرای قاپەگەی خوەیە

The more acidic the vinegar, the worse for its chalice

**Siqan neyde weri xer, key keyde weri sey**

سقان نەیدە وەر خەر، کەی کەیدە وەر سەی

Puts bone in front of the donkey, hay in front of the dog

**Sûk biçû, siLamet bewrew**

سووک بچوو، سلّامەت بەورەو

Travel light, return safe

**Sed bertîl, qerzig pasa nîyekey**

سەد بەرتیل، قەرزگ پاسا نییەکەی

Hundred briberies will not pay a single loan

**Serim bişkin, nirxim neşkin**

سەرم بشکن، نرخم نەشکن

Smash my head but not my price

**Seri me keçel u têxi tu birra**

سەرێ مه کەچەل و تێخ تو برا

My head is bald and your razor sharp

**Serê ki ser lê xefya, ta serê neçû ser nîyexefnê**

سەرێ ک سەر لێ خەفیا، تا سەرێ نەچوو سەر نییەخەفنێ

One who is accustomed to people bending their neck for him, will not himself bend the neck until he loses it

**Seg büd biray büçig neüd**

سەگ بۆد برای بۆچگ نەۆد

Rather a dog than little brother

**Seng u tirazü şerm le kes nîyekey**

سەنگ و ترازۆ شەرم له کەس نییەکەی

The scale is ashamed of no one

**Sey eray xawinmaL dûsê dîrin**

سەی ئەرای خاونمالْ دووسێ دیرن

People like the dog for the host's sake

**Sey har bû, quli maL-xawin girê**

سەی هار بوو، قول مالْخاون گرێ

A rabid dog bites its owner's leg

**Sey har imrê çill şewe**

سەی هار ئمرێ چل شەوه

A rabid dog lives for forty days

**Sey hegi pas keyd, nûrêde düya xwey**

سەی هەگێ پاس کەید، نوورێده دۆیا خوەی

The barking dog looks back

**Sêf (sêw) we sewzî neken, eger birresê xwey kefê**

سێف وه سەوزی نەکەن، ئەگەر برەسێ خوەی کەفێ

Do not pick the apple when it is green, it will fall by itself when it matures

# Ş

**Şêr wexti pîr bû, rûwa wepê exenê**

شیر وەختێ پیر بوو، رووا وه پێ ئەخەنێ

When the lion becomes old, it gets ridiculed by the fox

**Şikar we şûn kuşyeyd**

شکار وه شوون کوشیەید

Game is killed on site

**Şîyerîki diz u refîqi qafiLe**

شییەریک دز و رەفیق قافلّە

Thief's partner and caravan's friend

**Şêri naw wêşe nêr u ma neyrê**

شێر ناو وێشه نێر و ما نەیرێ

The lion in the grove has no male or female
[A lion is a lion]

**Şêt bû ta aşiq neüd (newd)**

شێت بوو تا ئاشق نەۆد

Be crazy so you do not fall in love

**Şîr daxe, pif le mas keyd**

شیر داخه، پف له ماس کەید

The milk is hot, he blows on the yoghurt

62

**Şêr şiknê, rûwî xwey (exwad)**

شێر شکنێ، رووی خوەی

The lion crushes, the fox eats


**Şeytan hersey firezane, tewqi naLet ha milê**

شەیتان هەرسەی فرەزانه، تەوقیٰ نالەت ها ملیٰ

Despite his knowledge the devil has a curse on him


**ŞewaL eray serdî u germî nîye**

شەوالٔ ئەرای سەردی و گەرمی نییه

Pants are not for heat and cold


**ŞewaL ayimi gêa (gida) le deri qingew dirryeyd**

شەوالٔ ئایم گیٔنیا لەدەر قنگەو دڕیەید

A poor man's trousers is torn at the back


**Şûxî wel minaLa meke, le cem xicaLetid keyd**

شووخی وەل منالٔا مەکه، له جەم خجالٔەتد کەید

Do not joke with a child, it will embarrass you publicly


**Şûwan wet: Eger me nîyatam, gurg rîyeneged xwardî**

شووان وەت: ئەگەر مه نییاتام، گورگ ڕییەنەگەد خواردی

The shepherd said: Had it not been for me the wolf
would have devoured your flock


**Şimşêri xas le qiLaf nîyemînê**

شمشێر خاس له قلٔاف نییەمینیٰ

A great sword does not stay in its sheath


**Şitir xawê düni, şitirelewan xawê**

شتر خاویٰ دۆنیٰ، شترەلەوان خاویٰ

The camel dreams a dream, the camel-herd another

**Şarid weten ya diLid weten?**

شارد وهتهن یا دڵد وهتهن؟

Is your city your homeland or your heart?

**Şelê minay kûrê kird**

شهلێ منای کووری کرد

The lame points out the blinds errors

**ŞewaL dirryay caw dünêde (le) xaw**

شهواڵ دریای جاو دۆنێده (له) خاو

The one who has torn trousers dreams of clothes

# T

**Ta cû tenge, biperri**

تا جوو تهنگه، بپهری

Jump the stream, while it is narrow!

**Ta zûre, qewaLe kûre [Ta zûr hes qewaLe betaLe]**

تا زووره قهواڵه کووره

As long as there is raw power, there will be no agreements!

**Tawbê gurg merge**

تاوبێ گورگ مهرگه

The wolf's remorse is death

**Tiway xwed binasî? Temaşa camek bike**

توای خوهد بناسی؟ تهماشا جامهک بکه!

Do you want to know yourself? Look in the mirror!

**Tu eger lawelawe zanî, xwed era xawdaw nayi?**

تۆ ئەگەر لاوەلاوه زانی، خوەد ئەرا خاوداو نای؟

Now, if you can sing a lullaby, why can't you sleep yourself?

**Ta peringe hes, era beyde aw?**

تا پەرنگه هەس، ئەرا بەیده ئاو؟

Why wade, if there is a crossing?

**Ta rûwî qewaLe da des, kewL u pûsê kenîn**

تا رووی قەواڵه دا دەس، کەوڵ و پووسی کەنین

Till the fox gave up the contracts, they had skinned it

**Ta aqiL rê rê kird, şêt perrîyew**

تا ئاقڵ ڕێ ڕێ کرد، شێت پەرییەو

While the wise took careful steps, the fool jumped over

**Tancî wexti şikar güyê tîyê**

تانجی وەخت شکار گۆیێ تییێ

The hunting dog want to crap when its time to hunt

**Tawisan bawgi gêas (gidas)**

تاوسان باوگ گنیاس

Summer is the poor's father

**Tancî we zûr bûweydê şikar, rîyeyde dar u binciga**

تانجی وەزوور بووەیدێ شکار، رییەیدەدار و بنجگا

If you force a hunting dog to hunt, it will crap everywhere

**Tirazû xêr u şerr**

ترازوو خێر و شەڕ

Scale: Blessing or misfortune

**Tirr we şewaLew (şûwaL) nîyewisê**

تڕ وه شەوالْو نییەوسێ

A fart is not stopped by the trousers

**Tu neüşe pêm bawgi segid – Ta xiraw nîyeme bawgi begid**

تو نەۆشه پێم باوگێ سەگد — تا خراو نییەمه باوگێ بەگد

Do not call my father dog and I will not swear at your esteemed father

**Tifê ki keydê hewa deyde naw demi çawi xwed**

تفێ ک کەیدێ هەوا دەیده ناو دەم چاو خوەد

If you spit upward you will get the spit in your own face

**Tûwas çiLmi bisirrê, çewi dirawird**

تووواس چڵمێ بسرێ، چەوێ دراورد

Tried to wipe his snot, blinded him

[Disservice]

**Tu ha bike mi hü kem, tu jin tîyerî me şü kem**

تو ها بکه م هۆ کەم، تو ژن تییەری مه شۆ کەم

You do this I do that, you take a wife, I'll take a husband

**Temaşaçî paLewane**

تەماشاچی پاڵەوانه

The spectator is brave

**Tewr dü xwey nîyetaşê (Tîşig dü xwey nawiri)**

تەور دۆ خوەی نییەتاشێ

The ax does not chop its own shank

**Tûway delakî we bani seri keçeLê minew yay bigrî?**

تووای دەلاکی وە بان سەر کەچەڵێ منەو یای بگری؟

You want to learn how to become a barber on my bald head's expense?

**Tîr u tîyet**

تیر و تیەت

Shot and stone

[Water and oil]

**Ta rezay xuda newd giLay dar nîyerizê**

تا رەزای خودا نەود گڵای دار نییەرزێ

Without God's permission the tree leaves will not fall

**Tîr xeyd, keman şarêdew**

تیر خەید، کەمان شاریدەو

Fires an arrow, hides the bow

**Tîke nanê le maLi xan hat, tütigê le şûni hat**

تیکه نانێ له ماڵ خان هات، توتگێ له شوونی هات

A piece of bread came from the Khan's house, it was accompanied by a puppy

[Luck followed by bad luck]

**Tîkey nan u pîyaLey çay, siqan azayî u patişayî**

تیکەی نان و پییاڵەی چای، سقان ئازایی و پاتشای

A piece of bread and a glass of tea - be healthy and feel like a king

**Ta nekîşî cefa, naynü sefa**

تا نەکیشی جەفا، ناينو سەفا

If you have not suffered through difficulties, you will not see any joy

[Per aspera ad astra]

# Ü

**Üşim le wirsî mirdim, üşê Besre xurma dîrê**

ئۆشم لە ورسی مردم، ئۆشێ بەسرە خورما ديرێ

I said: I'm dying of hunger, he said: There are plenty of dates in Basra

# W

**We desi xwem, agir nîyame qiji xwem**

وە دەسێ خوەم، ئاگر نييامه قژ خوەم

With my own hands, I burned my own hair

**We rûwa eyjin: Kî şahid tune? Eyji dumim**

وە رووا ئەيژن: کی شاهد تونه؟ ئەيژێ دومم!

They asked the fox: Who is your witness? My tail!

**Wetne pişî güyeged dermane, çü şardêwa**

وەتنه پشی گۆيەگەد دەرمانه، چۆ شاردێوا

They told the cat its stool is medicine, the cat hid it

**We meclis çîn asane, eLsanê girane**

وە مەجلس چين ئاسانه، ئەڵسانێ گرانه

It is easy to attend a meeting, difficult to leave

**Wexti şûwan nîye, biznegerrge edêde şûwan**

وەختێ شووان نییه، بزنەگەرگه ئەدێده شووان

When the shepherd is gone, the mangy goat is shepherd

**Wa le kuçig çiştê nîyewey**

وا له کوچگ چشتێ نییەوەی

Wind has no effect on the stone

[Sticks and stones may break my bones, but words will never hurt me]

**Wiraz le merreze tûrya, çill men we merreze zîyay kirya**

وراز له مەرمزه تووریا، چل مەن وه مەرمزه زییای کریا

The swine sulked and left the rice field, harvest increased by four hundred kg

**Wirsî nan dünêde xaw, birêne (birehnê?) caw**

ورسی نان دۆنێده خاو، برێنه جاو

The hungry man dreams of bread, the naked of clothes

**Wet: Le kû qurb eLgirtî? Wet le maLi xwem – Wet: Le kû le desê day? Wet le maLi xwem**

وەت: له کوو قورب ئەلگرتی؟ وەت له مالْ خوەم – وەت: له کوو له دەسێ دای؟ وەت له مالْ خوەم

Where did you enjoy respect? In my own house!
Where did they lose their respect for you? In my own house!

**We tinafi mift, xwey tasnê**

وه تناف مفت، خوەی تاسنێ

Hangs himself with a worthless rope

**We tin têjî kar nimew meyser – We zûwani şîrîn mar meyû we der**

وه تن تێژی کار نمهو مهیسهر – وه زووان شیرین مار مهیوو وه دهر

A job will not be finished with curtness - With smooth talk you get the snake out of its lair

**We çew dünê, we diL bawer nîyekey**

وه چهو دۆنێ، وه دڵ باوهر نییهکهی

He sees with his eyes, but do not believe in his heart

**We çewe azage deyd, we çewe kûrege sênêd**

وه چهوه ئازاگه دهید، وه چهوه کوورهگه سێنێد

He gives with the healthy eye and takes back with the blind

**Wextê diL pake, zûwan bîbake**

ومختێ دڵ پاکه، زووان بیباکه

Clean conscience, fearless tongue

**Werr we lay tenikyew dirryeyd**

وهر وه لای تهنکیهو درریهید

The coat ruptures in its thinnest part

**We dûsi taze u maL taze bawer meke**

وه دووس تازه و ماڵ تازه باوهر مهکه

Do not believe in a new friend and in a newly formed family

[Don't be naive]

**We rê kirdin çü ga, we aw xwardin çü xer**

وه رێ کردن چۆ گا، وه ناو خواردن چۆ خهر

Walk like a bull, drink like a donkey

**We zineyîm neym (nedîm) ciftê kewş le pay – Wexti mirdinîy deh (dîye) cift kewş le lay**

وه زنهییم نهیم (نهدیم) جفتێ کهوش له پای – وهخت مردنیی ده (دییه) جفت کهوش له لای

Throughout his life, I did not see his feet in a pair of shoes - When he died, there were dozens of shoes at his side

**Wexti kar u bar bûme yar – Wexti çiz u biz keydeme diz (mage)**

وهختی کار و بار بوومه یار – وهخت چز و بز کهیدهمه دز

When you need me, I am your friend - When you eat, you call me thief
[Ungratefulness]

**Wetne keçeL süre, wet: We me çe?**
**Wetin süri tune, wet: We tu çe?**

وهتنه کهچهل سۆره، وهت: وه مه چه؟
وهتن سۆری تونه، وهت: وه تو چه؟

They told the bald, it's wedding, he said: What is it to me?
They said: It's your wedding, he said: What is it to you?

**Wey hegi bay, we yekê u dûwan nîyewisê**

وهی ههگی بای، وه یهکێ و دووان نییهوسێ

An accident never comes alone
[When it rains, it pours]

# X

**Xuda xer enasî, şax epê neda**

خودا خەر ئەغاسی، شاخ ئەپێ نەدا

The Creator knows his donkey that is why he didn't gave it horns

**Xew le merg birdîye**

خەو لە مەرگ بردییە

Sleep is the little death (Sleep takes from death)

**Xefet mi xwey, mi xefet nîyexwem**

خەفەت م خوەی، م خەفەت نییەخوەم

You mourn for my sake? I do not mourn!

**Xer we ga üşê: Ti nefamî**

خەر وە گا ئۆشێ: ت نەفامی

The donkey said to the bull: You are stupid!

**Xawin şene, qatir senê!**

خاون شەنە، قاتر سەنێ!

He owns nothing, buys a mule!

**Xuda karê bisazê – xaLû xwarza bixwazê**

خودا كاری بسازی – خاڵوو خوارزا بخوازی

May the creator make the uncle (mother's brother) like his niece!

**Xuda genim diris keyd, xetê neyde beynîyan**

خودا گەنم درس كەید، خەتێ نەیدە بەینییان

When the Creator created the wheat; He put a dividing line at its centre

**Xan le xanime**

خان له خانمه

Behind every great man stands a woman

**Xuda lane eray baLdarê kûr diris keyd**

خودا لانه ئەرای باڵدارێ کوور درس کەید

God arranges for the blind bird

**Xuda le suLtan zûrdartire**

خودا له سوڵتان زووردارترە

God is mightier than the Sultan

**Xuda hegi tûway rizqi mûrîj bûrê, baL deyde pê**

خودا هەگێ تووای رزق موورێژ بوورێ، باڵ دەیدە پێ

When the creator wants to humble an ant, he gives it wings

**Xweri şewekî le êware tîjtire**

خوەر شەوەکی له ئێوارە تیژترە

Morning sun is sharper (stronger) than the midday sun

**Xweş-ferman şîyerîk dewLemene**

خوەشفەرمان شییەریک دەوڵەمەنه

The percipient is the rich mans partner

**Xetne sunete ne le bêxa**

خەتنه سونەته نه له بێخا

Circumcision is tradition, don't cut it all

**Xwem hüç nîyim, xaLûm minêde şêr**

خوەم هۆچ نییم، خاڵووم منێدە شێر

I myself am nothing; my uncle is like a lion

**Xwey dirrêd u xwey dürnêd**

خوەی دریَد و خوەی دۆرنێد

Tears it himself, sews it himself


**Xer barê tifeng bû, gurg xweydey**

خەر بارئ تفەنگ بوو، گورگ خوەیدەی

Even if the donkey's load is rifles, the wolf will eat it anyway


**Xeri karwançî çax nîyew**

خەر کاروانچی چاخ نییەو

A caravaneer's donkey don't become fat


**Xer gurg dünê, gûş qüçnê**

خەر گورگ دۆنێ، گووش قۆچنێ

If the donkey sees a wolf, it will put it ears backward


**Xas bû, xwem kerdenî – Xiraw bû Xuda kerdenî**

خاس بوو، خوەم کەردەنی – خراو بوو خودا کەردەنی

If it was good it was I – IF it was bad it was God


**Xeri leng düyay qafiLes**

خەر لەنگ دۆیای قافلەس

The lame donkey limps behind the caravan


**Xerrê ki le me çî – agir barê bû**

خەرئ ک لە مە چی – ئاگر بارئ بوو

The donkey I (got rid of) lost - May its load be fire


**Xerrê ki we pîyazê bisênîdey, le xergaw mirdaLa bû**

خەرئ ک وە پییازئ بسێنیدەی، لە خەرگاو مردالا بوو

A donkey bought for an onion, dies in the mud

# Y

**Ya pişt pirr, ya mişt pirr**

یا پشت پر، یا مشت پر

Either plenty of patrons or plenty of money

**Ye rîş u ye qeyçî**

یه ریش و یه قهیچی

Here you have the beard and here you have scissors

**Yekê agir çü le maLê, yekêtir melüçig we pê birşan**

یهکێ ئاگر چۆ له مالێ، یهکێتر مهلۆچگ وه پێ برشان

One man's house was ablaze, the other grilled a sparrow over the fire

# Z

**Zigi wirsî xün key**

زگ ورسی خۆن کهی

A starving stomach bleeds

**Zimsan yey şew bimînê, kari xwey keyd**

زمسان یهی شهو بمینێ، کار خوهی کهید

If the winter stays for one night only, it will do its job anyway

**Zûri xerr nîyetyê, zûr keyde paLan**

زووری خهر نییهتیێ، زوور کهیدهپالان

He can not control the donkey, so he tackles the saddle

**Zig deyde çeqû**

زگ دەیدە چەقوو

Gives the belly to the knife

[Person who is looking for trouble]


**Zêw sexte, ga we ga tawan girê**

زێو سەختە، گا وە گا تاوان گرئ

The earth is hard to plough; the bull blames the other bull

# Glossary

## A

**ALûş** Itch

**Amûza** Father's brother's son, Cousin

**Asîyaw** Mill

**Aş** Soup, Broth

**Aşkira** Visible, Open

**Aw heLgirê** Ripens, Matures

## B

**BaLdar** 1 Bird 2 Winged

**Bar** Burden, Load

**Barîkî** Thinness

**Besre** City in Iraq

**Bawanî** Dowry

**Bawejin** Brother's wife

**Beg** 1 Big 2 Powerful 3 Esteemed person

**BeLa** Accident, Calamity

**BeLam** But

**BeLm** Straw

**Benna** 1 Architect 2 Builder

**Berd** 1 Stone 2 Released

**Berr** 1 To bear fruit 2 A reddish stone 3 Barren, Empty

**Bertîl** Bribe

**Berü** Acorns

**Beşker** Distributor

**BetaLa** Unemployed

**Betir** Worse

**Beü** Bride

**Bewrew** Come back

**Bê-beş** Without share

**Bêcge** Except

**Bêgane** Stranger

**BêL** Shovel

**Bêx** Bottom

**Bidray** Pulled out

**Bijye** Live!

**Birayî** Brotherhood

**Birêne** Naked

**Birra** Sharp

**Birşan** Grilled

**Birüye** Eyebrow

**Bixt** Defamation, Accusation

**Biznegerrge** Shabby goat

**Bîbak** Fearless

**Bîbira** One who has no brothers

**Bîgar** 1 Idle 2 Empty handed

**Bîla** Allow, Let be

**BîxisLet** Characterless

**Bûrre** A cow's cry

**Bûşey** Milk it!

## C

**CahiL** Young

**Cam** Bowl

**Caw** 1 Clothes 2 Shroud

**Cefa** 1 Hardship 2 Coercion

**Cem** 1 Gathering 2 Gathered

**Cewr** 1 Hardship 2 Repression

**Ciftyar** Farmer

**Cîya** 1 Apart, Separate 2 Single

**Cîye cengan** Battleground

**Cû** Brook, Rivulet

**Cûwanî** Youth
**Cüye** Rye

## Ç

**Çarenüs** 1 Destiny 2 God
**Çem** Stream
**Çemya** 1 Kneeled 2 Bended
**ÇepLe** Clap
**ÇeqeL** Jackal
**ÇiLm** Snot
**Çinar** Maple
**Çiz u biz** Stomach (animals)
**ÇukuLşikin** 1 Hypocrite 2
Dishonest person
**Çuner** Beetroot
**Çü** Like, As

## D

**Da** 1 Mother 2 Wet-nurse 3
Gave
**DaL** 1 Vulture, Necrophagous
2 Place, Domain 3 Place in
the queue
**Dan** 1 Fodder 2 Seed 3 Each 4
Animal fat 5 Part, Share 6
Suffix with the meaning
Contain
**Danüke** Seed for the birds
**Dar u binciga** Bush
**Darizyê** 1 Rots 2 Crumbles
**Dawan** Bosom, Lap
**De** 1 Of 2 From 3 By
**Dem** 1 Mouth 2 Lit
**Demi çaw** Face
**Deng u bas** Discussion
**Deng** Call, Sound
**Derwes** Closed, Locked

**Desxirre** Betray and
deceive
**Dewa** Medicine, Cure
**DewLemen** Rich
**Dey** Village
**Dêan (digan)** Tooth
**Dêan saz** Dentist
**DêwiL** Drum
**DiL pak** Pure of heart, Clean
conscience
**Dilêr** 1 Brave 2 Hero
**Direw** 1 Reap 2 Harvest
**Dirêxt** Doubt, Hesitate
**Dirrêd** Tears, Demolishes
**Dirrig** Thorn
**Dît** (You) Saw
**Dûzex** Hell
**Dü** 1 Smoke 2 Tail
**DükeL** Smoke
**Dünê** Sees
**Dür** Far away, Distant
**Dürnêd** Sews
**Düyay** 1 After 2 Then, Later
**Düyet** Daughter

## E

**ELeng eLeng** Slowly
**ELis** Stand up
**Enaze** Measure, Size
**Erwawî** Agriculture
**Espi bidew** 1 Fast steed 2
Disciplined horse
**EşxaL** Cattle
**Ewsa** 1 Then 2 Later 3
Before
**Ez** I

## Ê

**Êwet** 1 Bring up 2 Foster, Breed

**Êyşa** Did hurt

## F

**Fêr** 1 Learn 2 Look, Seek

**Fêrege** The wise one, The competent one

**FiLanî** Somebody

**Fire** 1 Many 2 Much

**Firexwer** Gluttonous

## G

**Gawan** Cowherd

**Gawanî** Work as a cowherd

**GemaL** Old dog

**Genim** Wheat

**Gerden** Neck

**Gewra** 1 Big 2 Magnate

**Gêa (Gida)** Beggar

**GiLa** Leaf

**Gird(ew)** Gathered

**Girin** 1 Catches 2 Takes

**Girinew** Put in plaster

**Girrme** Rumble

**Girrme hirr** Flash and thunder

**Giry(êg)** Knot, Splice

**Gîrê** Cries

**Gîrfan** Pocket

**Gîwe** Shoe

**Gîweker** Shoemaker

**Gîya** Plant

**Gumra** One who is lost

**Gunakar** Sinner

**Gûçan** Stick withe bended handle

**Gûr** Calf

**Gûştxwer** Carnivore

## H

**Hakim** Judge

**HamaL** Competitor

**Har** 1 Rabid 2 rabies stricken

**Hegi** 1 When ... becomes 2 When ... is

**Hekîm** Doctor

**HeLeLe** Advertisement

**HeLing** Vulture

**HeLpeLe** 1 Nightmare 2 Mayhem, turbulence

**HeLperge** Kurdish folk dance

**HeLsê** Rise!

**Heres** 1 Prune 2 Breath 3 Avalanche

**Hersey** 1 When ... is 2 Even if, Despite

**HewL** 1 Worried for ... 2 Confusion 3 Load 4 Greed

**HewLe(ge)** 1 Load 2 Beast of burden 3 Towel

**Hewsa** Neighbor

**Heya** Shame

**Heyadar** Decent

**Hil** Without horns, Hornless

**Hin** Belongs to, Owned by

**Hisar** Yard

**Hûkare** 1 Addict 2 Used to 3 Trained

## I

**Işkeft** Cave

**Ixtîyar** 1 Choice 2 Authority

## Î

**Îse** Now, Just now

## J

**Jenê** 1 Play (Musical instrument) 2 Shakes
**Jeng** Rust
**Jijû** Hedgehog
**Jin mirdê** Widower

## K

**Karga** 1 Factory 2 Workshop
**Karwançî** 1 Caravaneer 2 Leader of a caravan
**Kase** 1 Turtle 2 Bowl
**Keftew** 1 Ignited 2 Started
**KeL girê** Mates
**KeL** Mountain goat
**KeLên** 1 Big, Massive 2 Magnate
**Keman** Bow
**Kem-beş** Small share
**Kemçig** Ladle
**Kemdesî** Poverty
**Kemtar** Hyena
**Kene** Water spring
**KewL u pûs** Skinn
**Key** 1 Hay 2 When
**Kêan (Keydan)** Haybarn
**Kirre** Crake
**Kîyerd** Dagger
**Kutek** Cudgel
**Kûrkûrek** Moth (Insect)
**Kûze** Pot
**Kûzeçî** Potter

## L

**La we la** 1 Walk sideways 2 Sideway
**Laf** Thick blanket
**Lane** Nest
**Lar** 1 Thin 2 Skew 3 Body 4 Prance 5 A kind of a rifle
**Lare(me)** Complaint
**Lawelawe** Lullaby
**Leng** Limping, Lame
**Lerr(ew)** Thin
**Lîqaw** 1 Saliva 2 Filtered rice water supposed to ease lung pains
**Lîtige** A kind of dessert made of flour, milk and water
**Luwîne** Miller
**Lüyet** Naked

## M

**MaL-birrya** 1 One whose home has been robbed 2 Robbed
**MaL-xawin** 1 Home owner 2 Landlord
**Mamir** Hen
**Mang** Moon
**Mange şew** Moonlight
**Margezyag** Bitten by a snake
**MawiL** Respite, Reprieve
**Maye** 1 Equity 2 Female 3 Cause
**Meçîr** Thread, String
**Meçit** Mosque
**Meçû** Don't go
**Mecükin** Don't cackle
**Mejenê** Plays (Musical instrument)
**Meke** Don't
**Mel** 1 Creature 2 Animal 3 Bird

**MeLaLikye** Don't beg
**Melüçig** Sparrow
**Men** Measurement unit equivalent to ten kilograms (Luristan)
**MenziL** Home, House
**Meres** Dog's necklace
**Merreze** Rice field
**Meşke** Water skin
**Mew** 1 Don't hit 2 Don't sting
**Mexwaz** Don't want to
**Mexwer** Don't eat
**Meyû** Comes
**Mêr** Man
**Mêz** 1 Urine 2 Table
**Mêze mêze** Need to pee
**Mi** I
**Mift** Free of charge
**Minakar** 1 One who forbids 2 One who points out errors
**Minêde** Looks like
**MirdaLa** Dies, Is killed
**Mirê** Dies
**Misewî** Mother's boyfriend
**Mişt** 1 Handful 2 Fist 3 Group 4 A part, a portion
**Miziney bigir** 1 Focus on 2 Focus! 3 Work with
**Mîr** Prince
**Mîrat** Inheritance
**Mîye** Ewe
**Mîyenê** Tire out
**Muflis** Bankrupt, Penniless

**Mûr** 1 Ant 2 Louse 3 Lamentation 4 Prayer stone 5 Seal
**Mûrî** Ant
**Müşim** I say

**N**

**NaLet** Curse, Damnation
**Namewq** Untimely, Whether appropriate or not
**Naşareza** Ignorant, Unaware
**Naweyn** 1 Between 2 Among 3 Border, Dividing line
**Newker** 1 Slave 2 Servant
**Ney(Nedî)** Didn't see
**Nezan** Ignorant, Fool
**Nêr** Male
**Nicaset** 1 Feces 2 Dirt
**Nijî** Lentil
**Nirx** Price
**Nîyefîsi** Don't soak
**Nîyekujyêdew** 1 Doesn't die 2 Is not quenched
**Nîyetaşê** 1 Doesn't shave 2 Doesn't shave (Wood)
**Nûkase** Newly rich
**Nû-Pa** Child who have recently learned to walk
**Nûrê** Looks, Sees
**Nûrr (Nûwirr)** Curse
**Nûrrê** 1 Looks 2 Looks at

**P**

**Pa pîya** Pedestrian
**Pacînge** Climbing holes
**PaL** 1 Press with the shoulder 2 Slope

**PaLan** A saddle for the donkey or the mule

**PaLewan** 1 Hero 2 Strong 3 From Pehle

**Pas** 1 Behind 2 Back side 3 Bark

**Pasa** Return the ...

**Paşne** Heel

**PeL** Boulder

**PeLe** Autumn rain

**PeLeng** Leopard

**Pelet** Rope

**PeLing** Leopard

**PêLa** Shoe

**Pen** 1 Advice 2 Proverb 3 Trick 4 Inappropriate behavior 5 Light (Weight)

**Peringe** 1 Crossing 2 Crossing in a river made by stones

**Pes (Pez)** Sheep

**Pêş** 1 Front 2 Front side

**Pif** 1 Blow 2 Fart

**Pile** 1 Degree 2 Stairway 3 Autumn rain 4 Floor 5 Category, Type 6 Movement

**Pirs** 1 Mourning ceremony 2 Question

**Pîran** 1 Oil lamps glass 2 Sad, Sorrowful 3 Sorry

**Pîrî** Old age

**PîyaLe** Glass

**Pîyawetî** 1 Chivalry 2 Courage, Valor 3 Integrity

**PîyeL** Bridge

**PûLadîn** Made of steel

**Pünge** Wild mint, Penny royal

## Q

**QafiLe** Caravan

**Qap** 1 Frame 2 Container

**Qatir** Mule

**Qayimî** Hardness

**QeLa** Crow

**QersequL** Donkey's droppings

**Qert** Loan

**QewaLe** 1 Contract, Agreement 2 Document, Record

**Qewr** Grave

**Qewr-ken** Gravedigger

**Qeyçî** Scissors

**Qeza** Misfortune, Calamity

**Qij** Hair of the head

**QiLa** 1 Fortress, Stronghold 2 Crow

**QiLaf** 1 Sheath, Case 2 Scabbard, A swords sheath

**QuLing** Pick, Pickaxe

**Qurb** 1 Esteem 2 Respect 3 Reputation

**Qüçne** Lays backward

**Qülinê** Crows

**Qüt** Swallow

## R

**Ras** 1 Straight 2 Right 3 Right (Direction) 4 Plane, Level

**Raw** Hunt

**Rehman** 1 God 2 Mercy, Compassion

**Req** 1 Hard 2 Dry 3 Frozen

**Resin** Rope
**Retinê** Roars
**Rewa** Allowed, Permitted
**Rewyad(ew)** 1 Lägger sig 2
Stops 3 Ends
**Rê rê kird** 1 Walked slowly 2
Hesitated
**Rixi eçê** Is afraid
**Rîşqenî** Ridiculed
**Rîyen** Flock of sheep
**Rrimnê** 1 Overthrows 2
Raze, Demolish
**Rûle** Dear, Beloved
**Rûwa** Fox
**Rûwî** Fox

**S**

**Saçû** Straight cane
**Salar** 1 Healthy
2 Supreme commander,
Leader
**Saman** 1 Blessing 2 Order,
Arrangement
**San** 1 Stone 2 King, Monarch
3 Whetstone 4 Place
**SawmaL** 1 Homeowner 2
Landlord
**Saz** Flute
**Sefa** Joy, Delight
**SeLamet** 1 Healthy, Well 2
Whole, In one piece
**Seng u men** Prerequisite
**Seng u tirazû** Scale, Wave
**Setmenî** One hundred
Toman (Iranian currency)
**Sewr** Patience
**Sey (Seg)** Dog

**Sêf (Sêw)** Apple
**Sênêd** Buys
**Sifredirr** Ungrateful
**SipLe** Stupid, Fool
**Siqan** Bone
**Siqan azayî** Good health
**Sirr** 1 Slippery 2 Very cold 3
Secret 4 Soundless, Mute 5
Lubricate 6 Numbness 7
Donkey's howl
**Sitr** 1 Secret 2 Reputation,
Honor 3 Sorcery
**Sûwar** Rider

**Ş**

**Şa-diz** King of thieves,
Extremely skilled thief
**Şardêwa** Hid it
**Şelîte** Shameless
**Şen** 1 Sand 2 Prank, Fun
**Şerm** 1 Decency 2 Be
ashamed 3 Shyness 4
Manners 5 Vagina
**Şerr** Problem
**Şesi xew** Dazed with sleep
**ŞewaL** 1 Underwear 2
Trousers
**Şewekyan** Morning hour
**Şêt** Nuts, Crazy
**Şêwya** 1 Mixed, Blended 2
Turmoil 3 A plan that is
thwarted
**Şikar** 1 Game, Quarry 2 Hunt
**Şiknê** 1 Breaks 2 Cracks
**Şirr** Old
**Şitir** Camel
**Şitirelewan** Camel-herd

**Şîre u yere** Cooperative
**Şîrî** Childhood
**Sunet** Tradition
**Şûwanî** Work as a shepherd

## T

**Taf** 1 Quick, Swift 2 Haste, Hurry
**TaLan** Plunder
**Tancî** 1 Hound 2 Greyhound
**Tane** 1 Pupil 2 Blame, Criticism 3 Discoloration in the eye
**Tarîf** 1Commendation, Praise 2 Definition 3 Tell about
**Tasnê** Suffocates
**Tawan** 1 Guilt, Blame 2 Wrong, Wrongdoing 3 Fine, Pay a fine
**Tawisan** Summer
**Tema** 1 Wish 2 Greed
**Temakar** Greedy
**Teng** 1 Distress 2 Tight, Narrow 3 Narrows 4 Hard tied
**Tep u tûz** Dust
**Tewn** Waving machine
**Tewq** 1 Wreath 2 Iron ring 3 Middle part
**Tewr** Axe
**Teyre** Thief
**Têr** Full, Satisfied
**Tike** 1 Drop 2 Portioned and grilled meat
**Tilanim** (I) Mashed, Squeezed, Crushed

**Tinaf** Rope
**Tiway** Wants
**Tîke** 1 Part, Share 2 Bite
**Tîr** 1 Arrow 2 Shot
**Tîşig** Axe
**Tîyerîke-şew** Dark night
**Tîyet** A large and smooth stone
**Tûk** 1 Shell, Skin, Peel 2 Dandruff 3 Tree bark
**TûkiLaş** 1 Wood chip 2 Bark
**Tûr** 1 Fool, Stupid 2 At loggerheads, disagreement 3 Net
**Tûrya** Sulked and went
**Tûway** 1 Wants 2 Wishes
**Tûz** Dust
**Tülekî** 1 Laughing-stock, Mockery 2 Cranium 3 Corny, Silly
**Türe** Sack, Bag
**Tütig** Puppy

## U

**Usa** Master, Expert

## W

**Wa** Wind
**Wade** 1 Commitment 2 Promise, Vow
**We cas** Is left, Remains
**Wefir** Snow
**Wehar** Spring (Seasons)
**Wene (Weger ne)** Or else
**Wer kefê** 1 Ends up in front 2 Evolves, Develops
**Wer** 1 Front 2 In front of
**Weren** Ram

**Werr** A kind of a "coat" made of the same material as Gilîm (Carpet made of goat's wool). It is not woven; it is compressed to the desired shape.

**Weten** 1 Homeland 2 Nation

**Weü** Bride

**Wey** 1 Bride 2 Birch

**Wiraz** Swine

**Wirsî** Hungry

## X

**Xan** 1 Khan 2 Ruler 3 Magnate

**Xanim** 1 Lady 2 Wife

**Xawin-MaL** 1 Homeowner 2 Landlord

**Xaye** 1 Testicle 2 Courage

**Xergaw** 1 Mud, Clay 2 Sludge

**Xerid** You buy

**Xetne** Circumcision

**Xêz** Wise

**Xişe** Rustle

**Xîş** Family

**XuLekû** Ash

**Xûwî** 1 Goodness 2 Good

**Xwazmenî** Marriage proposal

**Xweş-ferman** Responsive, Attentive

**Xweş-hisaw** Generous

**Xwey** 1 Eats 2 Himself, Herself, Itself

## Y

**Yey lawa** Suddenly, Sudden

## Z

**Zanû** Knee

**Zat** 1 (in) Mind 2 Bravery 3 Existence

**Zel** Reed

**Zerr** Gold

**ZewaL** 1 Burden 2 Enemy

**ZiLm** Injustice

**Zinê** Alive, Living

# References

- **Ferhengî başûr** , Pûrsman publishing house, 2006 by **Ebbas Celîlîan** (عباس جلیلیان)
- **Zerîne u sîmîne 3**, PDF format, not published, by **Ebbas Celîlîan** (عباس جلیلیان)
- **www.feyli.se**